36P

Prelude to a Marriage

Letters & Diaries

of

John Coulter & Olive Clare Primrose

Oberon Press

ISBN 0 88750 293 8 (hardcover)
ISBN 0 88750 294 6 (softcover)

Printed in Canada

PUBLISHED IN CANADA BY OBERON PRESS

For Babs' colleague
and faithful friend
Peggy Blackstock

The cover portraits are of John Coulter and Olive Clare
Primrose at the time of their engagement. Both were made
in London, the former in 1936, the latter a year earlier.

1

Before I met the Canadian poet, Olive Clare Primrose, I had not seriously contemplated marriage, nor ever had the least intention of leaving Ireland and London to become a Canadian citizen. But I did marry and did become a Canadian citizen. To recall the why and the how of it now, nearly forty years later, promises diversion which I much need, and even pleasure; and if in reading it there should perhaps be some pleasure for others as well as for me, so much the better. It is a story I am not ashamed to call a love-story—a true-love story: true love from the beginning for me, but it became mutual true love only in time.

We met on Saint Valentine's Day, 1928, in London, in the Cursitor Street office of the literary quarterly *The New Adelphi* which I then managed as assistant to John Middleton Murry, its editor. I have described that meeting in my memoirs *In My Day*, but not the long journey through cloud and sun, years of stress and strain, heartbreak and uncertainty, an ordeal that brought us at last to happiness such as neither of us had believed to be possible. The dry, laconic day-by-day record of fact which is in my diaries, the from-time-to-time evocation of mood and impulse which is in her journals—her intimate communings with herself—these, with whatever of narration I must add, together with the letters we exchanged during the desolate year when she had returned to Canada and I had remained, are the substance of this story.

The seven years of uncertainty between our first meeting and the time of our coming together I shall pass over, for they were years of distress and pain which I have no wish to relive. The circumstances of my life, economic and personal, were such that, however nagging and unremitting my desire I could not honourably and with any belief that I might succeed, press my suit on Primmy (as I had come to call her). She herself was tossed about and torn between conflicting loyalties and passions—passions being not too strong a name for the feelings which attached her to her Canadian family, particularly to the tragically bereaved four children of the person she had loved best on earth, her elder sister Dorothy, Dorothy Joy, whom she called her "sunflower weary of time"; and to her country, particularly her parents' island Dahwamah, in the Muskoka lakes where she had summered from infancy, and which she referred to as "a place called Paradise." These loyalties and passions constantly conflicted with an urge to separate herself so that she might become the poet she believed herself to be, conflicted with a longing to become part of the literary life of London; and with this there were intermittent spells of illness, one of which was dangerous enough to detain her for most of one winter in a Canadian sanatorium for TB—the disease that killed the writer whose work she devotedly admired, Katherine Mansfield.

Toward the end of 1934 I had ceased to be more than tangentially associated with *The New Adelphi*, now again *The Adelphi*, which Middleton Murry had set up in part as a memorial to Katherine Mansfield, and in the office of which Primmy had worked for a time as my assistant. She was again in London. I, too, had come back to London from one of my frequent sojourns in Belfast—had come back because of work for the BBC which entailed research in the Reading Room of the British Museum. I was now determined to be with Primmy as frequently and for as long as possible—determined somehow to find a way of transforming what had simmered so long in my heart as no more than a sort of tacit engagement into a firm commitment to get married. Primmy had taken for herself a small bed-sitting room at the top of 32 Dorset Square, Baker Street. It had a small window overlooking the gardens, and there she and I were to be together. There, in her journal, under the date Friday, 23 November, 1934, she confided to herself:

This is a moment, always, of peace and reckoning. I love this little room. . . . On armistice night he was here. We came to a rather funny conclusion—characteristic of us. . . .

I remember what it was: a repetition of the phrase in which we had once made that tacit engagement: that we should get married "if and when," meaning if and when it should ever become possible. A poor start to my final sortie, but at least an acknowledgement that she herself knew what I was up to. Her journal continues:

I sat at his feet on the floor, and he examined my brace-lets, and then bent my hand backwards and folded it forward in his. . . .

That moment is as vivid in my memory as if it had happened last night. She was wearing over her shoulders a green silk square, emerald green perhaps in compliment to me. It was part of the uniform of Havergal College, her Toronto school. She called it her "Havergal square." It beautifully set off her heavy, bobbed, black hair, which I loved. And when she looked up at me I noticed and loved the extraordinarily wide pupils of her eyes which were grey with a touch of brown, and noticed the width of of her forehead and her pointed chin and a mouth that had no hint of meanness. I told her what moved me. I longed to stay with her then, all night. But it was not to be. She has written of it:

(He said) "I must go."
"Well—if you must, pull me up."
I held out my hands and he pulled me to my feet and

7

took me in his arms. Gently then he kissed me. He seemed very tall. It was a gentle kiss, quite unhurried and yet not everlasting, gently insistent like a tender naive experiment.

"I try to understand you," said John. "I try to understand you but something gets in the way. I can't."

I was aware of something elusive, withheld, in her. Something I could not fathom, beyond artifice, not to do with feminine wiles. It was our first kiss.

Now to anticipate a question likely to occur to those who read these pages, I must with some reluctance divulge what it was that for a time prevented Primmy and me from feeling free to come and go as we pleased. I was involved in a prolonged, most delicate and difficult process of disentangling myself from an attachment to an old and very dear friend, the painter James Sleator. It was an attachment which had passed beyond admiration of person and of talent, and deepened into affection, but affection short of love. There had also been the binding of shared living expenses, of rent and food and the like, and those consolations engendered by mutual trust and the intimacies of life together.

Primmy, too, had been living with a dear friend, the actress Molly Jones who bore a captivating facial resemblance to Greta Garbo. Her stage name was Anne Hayward. Primmy greatly admired Molly, and was stimulated by her ironic wit and knowledge of the world and of London's West End in particular. But from an urge to be more completely herself she had now moved into quarters of her own and was finding readjustment difficult.

Unfortunately, for me at least, the process of disentangling was resented, unreasonably, bitterly resented, betraying an intolerable and dangerous degree of possessiveness and jealousy that extended to threats, even physical threats, desperate stratagems to prevent my meeting Primmy, a sustained distressing struggle to stave off and destroy what was developing between her and me. I was convinced that both for Jimmy's sake and my own the time had come to break, but not abruptly. I had all-too-convincing reason to believe that an abrupt break—even if loyal considerateness for all that had been had not forbidden it—might result in driving my old companion into a state of at least temporary insanity, if not into committing some overt act of violence against his nature and possible only in a moment of insanity. Hence the obligation to avoid the harshness of a direct break, to use instead every resource of tact, forebearance and flexibility of which I was capable.

Of this predicament, even on that evening of decision, November 11, I had not yet felt free to tell Primmy; nor had she told me of whatever of a similar nature she may have been experiencing in however more civilized, less extreme form. Hence the puzzlements, bewildered wonderings, at my seeming inconstancy which will appear in extracts from her self-communings during the months that followed.

It chanced that I had almost at once to go back to Belfast —to write for the Northern Ireland station of BBC a Christmas Tree program, and a feature-program series, *Tales of the Towns*. I did speak of this to Primmy, as she reminds herself on Monday, 17 December:

> Met J at the British Museum at 12. We walked and talked. Had a sherry and, later, sandwiches and tea. Re his staying "a bit" in Ireland . . .

I told her I should have to be away for a bit in Ireland, but that Mac (the painter Dolly McKibben, who was to paint a portrait of Primmy which was exhibited in the Paris Salon and illustrated in *La Revue Moderne*) frequently

9

visited her family who lived not far from my mother's house. I suggested, as Primmy went on to record:

"You'd have to come and stay with McKibben for a bit. Or I'd take a cottage down by C . . . [Comber, near Strangford Lough]. Would you come, Primmy?"
"I might," said I, with a crooked grin.

But because of the implications of that "crooked grin" as I interpreted them, along with difficulties in having her with me in Ireland at that time, I dropped the subject. So, in her journal for 21 December.

But he did—I suppose—slide off to Ireland without a word. *I don't know what to do.*

She went to Bognor Regis with her actress friend, Molly, and during the first weeks of the new year, 1935, we had to put up with knowing no more of each other than could be gleaned from a few scribblings—postcards and letters.

By mid-January I was again in London. On Tuesday the 29th I was to dine as their guest with Primmy and Molly Jones. I was to join them at 6.30. I thought best to say so openly to Jimmy Sleator, when it was six o'clock and time to leave the studio. At least for once to tell of those resentments and stratagems of which I have spoken, here as an example is what then happened. Instantly abristle with hostility, Jimmy went to the front door, bolted the inside lock, put the key, the only one, in his pocket and as he came back, said "You're not going." As I had decided beforehand that on all such occasions, if they should occur as I felt sure they would, I should not permit myself to be trapped by violence into violence, I said nothing, did nothing. I simply sat down and sat silent, making no move. He pretended not to notice. Yet it was impossible not to notice since the tension between us was all but palpable, a thing not to be endured; the agony of it continued, but instead of finding relief in some outburst the tension and first fury gradually became dispersed and ended, for Jimmy, in a state of distress, a simmering in futile exasperation. Half an hour passed. I knew that now Primmy and Molly would be expecting me to arrive at any moment. But I still waited, sitting without a move, without a word. Another fearful half hour passed. The clock struck seven. Jimmy walked to the door, put the key in the lock, left it there, and came back into the studio without looking at me or saying a word. Without a word I went out and on to make my apologies to Primmy and Molly, concocting as I went some explanation for my long delay. Such was but the first of a succession of painful scenes which happened during the months that followed; nights on which after being with Primmy I did not go back to the studio but instead would wander about the streets seeking composure and then would go, perhaps for several days and nights to some place, lodging-house, doss house or hotel. That night, I slept in a small back room of the Royal Hotel —just managing to avoid the misery of a later occasion when, having indignantly walked out of the studio with hardly more than a bus fare in my pocket I had the sharply enlightening and saddening experience of spending a most miserable night bedded among the derelicts and down-and-outs in a house of shelter somewhere behind King's Cross railway station which, if I remember rightly, was called Hampden Club.

Shortly after that revealing incident of the locked door I felt obliged to tell Primmy something of the predicament, and of my circumstances generally. For that purpose I went to her on a Sunday forenoon to Dorset Square. She had just had breakfast—the token breakfast which, with luncheon and dinner of hardly more than yogurt and orange juice— seemed to be her daily fare. She was resolutely slimming, and was not far from her aim of appearing, as she mockingly described it, like "two boards slapped together." She had bathed, and was in an attractive dressing-gown of soft green with white facings. I took her to the nearby Tussaud's restaurant—for being Sunday morning few others were open—and told her the uninspiring truth, as much of it and with as much candour as I dared without risk of frightening her off—the truth about Jimmy; but also about my family, in particular about my responsibility to what remained of it, my widowed mother and unmarried sister. Primmy listened, quietly and attentively. She said little. Yet though I was warmed and encouraged by her manifest if unspoken sympathy I saw that she was seriously perturbed. We went back to her place and talked it over. Before I left I heard her say, almost in a whisper yet meant for me to hear, "I guess I'm not going through with this." Momentarily I was dismayed—but momentarily because as we parted I heard her for the first time murmur the endearment "darling,"— an endearment which, however commonplace in the chatter of that time, sprinkled about like powdered sugar in West End comedies, was with her no such fortuitous throwaway term.

What was in her mind she confessed to herself in her journal, Saturday, 23 February.

> I sat on the floor this morning in front of the fire. . . . The window framed blue sky—the blue sky of spring— and the top of the trees in Dorset Square. I thought . . . I'm going where the sky is nearly always blue.

And a few days later she continued:

> Warily, from a long way off I see complications growing like hardy weeds. . . . A disturbing evening, troubling my sleeping conscience. . . . I sat disgruntled in every *fibre*

of my being, on the floor. Even sleep has deserted me. . . .
The truth of the matter is that I am in a sticky place . . .
I cannot move, and I am lost in any case. All familiar
props are missing and, though something, it is of no
material use that J should hold me in his arms and quote,
"I dare not think of thee. . . ." And the lovely end, "I
run, I run, I am gathered to thy heart." I felt awed, posi-
tively, to think that J, a man of his mentality, had been
saying *that* to me. I felt depressed.

She then quotes to herself:

"All things are possible to him who believes: they
are less difficult to him who hopes, they are easy to him
who loves, and simple to any who do all three."
—Brother Lawrence

But she had not yet managed this simplicity. Indeed she
presently resumes:

I find it is far more dangerous than it appears. He
seems so savagely depressed and doubts me so appal-
lingly. . . . That gloomy, creaking voice. Oh my poor J
it is not, believe me, the way.

I knew it, and knew that with what I was going through
at the studio I could not and had not the least intention to
effervesce like some verbal-champagne-bubbler in a Noel
Coward comedy.

Sanguinary in mind and body I feel. I'm *not* in love
with him. He's so gloomy! He's so gentle! But I am
obsessed by him, and I want to know why. I am *every*
night too sleepy to think it out; in the morning too depressed; and by day too distrait . . . too distracted. In any

case the result is I shy away from it ... I have *no* place at all. ...

A pair of arms is all the place I want. Shall I marry J? Spend a few enlightening nights with J? Or merely—sail away ... after a few more tender passages?

Three courses. A few days later, on 2 April, she tells herself of the decision she has made between them:

J telephoned tonight. A long lecture on my loafing. But I was gentle and submissive and exceeding sad. Yet when I heard him, those three "courses" perished like mists before sun. Only "to sail away" remained. Nor am I as relieved as I expected to be. I am *sad*.

Beside desire to evade an unequivocal commitment to marry me, other considerations strengthened her decision to sail away: Norman Macdonnell, husband of her sister Agnes (she was affectionately known as Jimmy), a Justice of the Supreme Court of Canada but a lively, bantering, witty teaser of Primmy, was gravely ill; recurring spells of feeling guilt about, as she put it in self-accusation, "deserting her children," her nephews and nieces, the four orphaned Joys; that powerful, insistent longing to be again in Canada among the woods and waters of her beloved island home.

She had confided to her journal Sunday, 3 April, 1935:

I see the moonlight, the dark wide waters, the black islands, the cold blinding glitter of the moon. I feel on my cheeks the unseen wind—a mysterious breath. I hear the light squish-squish-bang of my little canoe, leaping into the moonlight out of the darkness, the wind-haunted darkness of the lake.

She consulted the sailing-lists—but the *early summer* sailings of liners she had sailed in: *Majestic, Berengaria, Bremen, Empress of Britain.* This forestalled precipitancy. It left time in which to allow the flowering thorn to unfold, if unfold it might. If this, for Primmy, was conscious policy, my awareness of it was no more than surmise. For she covered up all signs of dejection in gaiety of spirit that was far more in her nature than descent into moods of melancholy and despair; moods which she wrote of and depicted in verse:

I dug love's grave and weeping said to him,
Here is your little kingdom all prepared. . . .

It was about the inevitable passing of youth and love. But —cover it up. With her diffidence and gentleness her laughter was what I most needed and loved. When of a morning I was on my way to the BBC we would meet at Baker Street station and, blithe as a pair of mayboys, go jaunting hand-in-hand along the Marylebone Road and by Portland Place to Broadcasting House. She would wait for me in the foyer, or in the nearby ABC tea shop; and then, my business with the program-people transacted, we would discuss it as we went back by the way we had come. But at York Gate we would turn off into Regent's Park. If we met cat or dog she could not refrain from stopping to speak to it and caress it. I remember one Great Dane which captivated her:

Walking home from the BBC we passed a Great Dane. The lovely brute beat that flail-like tail and even stretched his great head amiably, answering my excess of admiration.

It was true. I had known no other person who seemed so

15

easily and happily at one with all the creatures, and they with her—all so-called dumb animals, except, indeed, certain of the more disagreeable because aggressive and acquisitive of her own species.

In the park we spent many mornings and many nights, happy to be with each other; in the morning walking by the crocuses and daffodils round the lake, to wander in the fields, finding there a place to lie in the sun, and for Primmy to take innumerable snapshots of the waterfowl and of the children at play, and of me. Borrowing her camera I took as many of her. At night when the park was closed we crossed the little bridge, "our bridge," from the Outer to the Inner Circle, and there, on the seats around the railings of the Queen's Gardens, we frequently sat talking for hours when the disarray in our affairs threatened to defeat us. On several occasions, sitting there or for variety rising and slowly walking the complete round of the Circle, we watched the grey of dawn widening over the trees and the lake, with waking waterfowl giving voice and thrush and blackbird beginning to sing. I would see a sleepy Primmy to Dorset Square and walk on, sometimes throwing up my hat, to whatever lodgings I had found for that night.

Primmy had been invited to sit for her portrait by her friend Mac. During the sittings I went betimes to Mac's studio in Duke Street, off Baker Street. I was to offer whatever comment I cared to make, but finding that this was one of the occasions when Primmy was, as she herself said, "paralyzingly shy," I said little. Later, Mac gave a party at which her work was to be seen by a few close friends: Molly Jones; Algy and Mary Bishop, who had met at Oxford and were both writers, Algy, an Englishman, having published a first novel, *Paper Kingdom*, and having with Mary— from the Canadian west—set up and for a time edited and heroically maintained in Toronto a little literary magazine *The Twentieth Century*.

16

Primmy's journal, Thursday, 20 April:

The oft-remarked "party" was duly thrown in Mac's big room. Owing to a fire it was held by candle-light, which charmed me.

The Bishes came, and J, slightly under protest. I left the candle-light flickering on Mac's portraits, sketches, and on a dimly effective canvas of me, like a Frans Hals in brigand hat—and went down to let J in. In the blessed darkness of the little narrow hall he caught me up and gave me a hurried, stolen, breathless sort of kiss.

The evening was fun, in a way. Mary talked too much, too loud, too fast and too long. I did the reverse, losing nothing and sitting, as J said, "With a sort of dusk about me." Algy and J talked—A with a sort of earnest relief. Here was *one* who spoke his own tongue. M got—so she says—tight and therefore a little expansive. Mac of course brooded happily sphinx-like. We toured her pictures, candle in hand. J likes mine, greatly.

He sat there, looking very long and thin and amused. That thin, angular face of his—mature, smiling. Suddenly I made a sort of snatch—mentally. You must not *lose this*, I cried to myself. At Mac's insistence I took him down, for at midnight, having considerably overstayed his allotted time, he left. In that little black hallway he put his arm round me, candle and all. I caught at his coat. "Don't go," I whispered. [In two more days it would be Good Friday, and for a little respite I had thought of leaving London, perhaps to spend Easter with my family in Belfast.]

"Say you won't go."

"I won't," he smiled.

As I went back to Edwardes Square, to the studio, I weighed the significance of that "Don't go" against the whispered, "I guess I'm not going through with this." But I could not persuade myself that the scales were other than in balance.

This had been confirmed by Primmy, to herself, as an entry in her journal, Thursday 15 April, makes clear.

It is still raining and blurring the tender green of the Square. I am still feeling, like the day, chilled and desolate.

J arrived about 12. He didn't leave till shortly after 4. Ah, I feel *exceedingly* desolate.

He no longer spars about. He takes me in his arms as soon as the door is shut behind him.

"Do you believe it now?" he said.

"Believe what?"

"That I love you."

"Yes."

"And you, Primmy?"

"I don't know. I only know I don't want to lose you."

"You'll never do that."

We had a picnic on the floor.

"I adore the lovely gentle spirit of you." See! It *is* the language, the language that one hears only rarely, rarely.

I was looking out . . . into the dim Square.

"Shall we go away tonight?" he asked me.

I shook my head.

I can't even remember the things he said, rainbow-coloured things, extravagant, that I gathered greedily into my overburdened arms, crying as I nursed them, "I will make a cloak of these against the dark and the cold and the winter." As near as I have ever been to loving him, then. . . . Here is, you know, a man. They are rare, remember: without lands or horses, encumbered with "family," hung with situations, mysterious—*here is a man.*

18

She had added a sort of postscript paragraph:

There was a sort of ecstasy about yesterday afternoon. God—I feel empty, drained and incredibly lonely and forlorn today. My firmament bristles with hostile stars.

Then—a feeling frequently expressed—about the act of writing these intimacies down, even in the privacy of her diary.

Forgive me, if I have murdered something lovely. Unfinished but lovely.
6.35 PM.
J has just been here.... He says that *this* has been more to him than anything in his life, and that that great Moloch the future, cannot wreck it.

Two days later the delicate up-and-down of the scales still preoccupied her:

All those bogey men that J so painfully erects, I look at them gravely. A mother and sister, eh? An empty cash-box, eh? A half-demented artist in love with an old companion, eh? And other weeds growing lustily in the garden. Oh, my poor John! I never think of them at all. I look at them with grave concern, and behind that I am thinking—almost—I love him. Do I *want* him?
And time marches on bringing the inevitable embarking nearer . . . nearer. . . . I feel terribly alone with this problem. I have got to take some step, perhaps the most fatally misguided of my life: I have got to leave—with no security of return—John.

That she had got to leave seemed to be the one certainty on which I could count, and I was determined that if indeed she was determined to "sail away," possibly not ever to return, I should, before being laid waste by this disaster, be with her at every moment that I could be free of work and of the wearing desperations into which days and nights at the studio had degenerated. I was poignantly aware, and said so to her, that this "now"—the two of us together for a few more weeks in London—was all we had with certainty, our one chance to brim up our lives with a happiness that might never be possible to either of us again. I proposed days in the country, nights at some country inn. I should have loved even a whole day together at Kew or Kenwood. I spoke of Kenwood. But Primmy—from some motive that I suspected had not to do with her own need or inclination, could not come. This suspicion seems confirmed by her journal:

> This was the day *I* thought we were going to spend among the Kenwood pools. . . . All through the lovely Wednesday, the lovely Thursday, gentle like summer— the air soft on your face—I thought, "I might be there with J on the green hills of Kenwood." And I mistrust the future as one does who has not lived the present. I could have had that long spring day. . . . *I* knew it wouldn't come again, and I was quite right, you see. For can the capricious English weather—God—draw more than two such days out of the bag? I could have spent the summer with you, John. . . . Only last Sunday he said,
> "The week shoots up in a flame when I see you. Like a crocus bursting out of the dull earth."
> And if I'm so fancy free why the divil do I gloom thus?
> How tired, how *tired* I am. I feel as "gai" as a mute at a funeral . . . as dead as if someone had died. I haven't the spiritual energy to "look forward."

I had sensed these dangerous lapsings into uncertainty

and despair with, in Primmy's case, their physical danger—
even after our happiest times together.

> J came at 1.30. We lunched . . . walked in the park
> . . . came back here. I took an axe and told him what I felt
> to be the case for he is talking of marrying.
>   He gathered me up in his arms and made love to me,
> gently. And at the end he said,
>   "You're a bit bewildered, aren't you?"
>   His gentleness and sweetness were my undoing.

I was myself a bit bewildered, and hurt, by her manifest
pleasure in our being together, coupled with her unwilling-
ness to give me assurance that her sailing away might not be
the end for us.

> Once when we were in the park he tried in vain to get
> me to swear I'd be back in the autumn. Petulantly I
> refused.
>   "God! And I did so want to have some sleep tonight,"
> he cried.

I could do no more than rely on my own resolve that I
should find some way round her reticences and reluctances.
I knew the painful schism in her affections, the crucial decision she was evading. If I could involve her in what was
most pleasant in my own comings and goings . . .
  I had been commissioned by the BBC to attend and report
on the round of weekly tennis tournaments which begins at
Bournemouth and culminates at Wimbledon. I greatly enjoyed these occasions—playing superbly, by proxy, a game
at which though I loved it I never excelled. I would ask
Primmy to come with me. The first she came to was the St.
George's Hill Club tournament at Weybridge.

All day with J. From 11.30. We went down to Weybridge on the 1.24 and came back on the 5.13. Saw Helen
Wills, and trees and ponds, and tennis courts—and us....

That was on the Monday, the opening day. I had been
feeling grim and depressed—one of the occasions of having
had to walk out of the studio after enduring a night and
morning of acrimonious onslaughts. Primmy had joined
me for breakfast at Shearn's vegetarian restaurant on Tottenham Court Road. Now, again, on the Friday, she came
with me.

Message from J. "Gone to Weybridge." "Damn," says
I. must follow 'um! But he missed the train. So, hand-in-
hand—"Come unto these yellow sands,"—we caught the
2.25. Rather lovely day, but cold, half-gale blowing.
Reached the Club about 3.15, and saw Helen Wills finish
off little (Billy?) Yorke. Saw also Buster Andrews, the
giant-killer; and saw J's face, and the cloud-hunted sun,
and the turbulent green things that blew and bowed and
bent in the half-gale, and the wind-curdled lily pond
spread and brimming below the long windows of the tea-
room.
Caught the 6.25 back—where I got the jim-jams and
coloured like an unhappy kid because of a carriage full of
louts. *Idiot!*

Our carriage, which we had hoped to have for ourselves,
was invaded by a gang of loutish youths, perhaps getting
home from their jobs at the end of their day. I was rather
amused by their gaucheries. I thought they were showing-
off a bit in our presence, but Primmy was uncomfortable
with it. Afterward she waited while I broadcast my comments on the tournament. Then we walked our customary
walk through Regent's Park, round by the Outer Circle to

22

Dorset Square. It was very late when I left—the morning's grimness and desperation all but forgotten in the happiness of the day.

But our day-of-days was to come. It was Whitsun weekend. I had gone to St. Leonard's, to my sister Annie and her husband Jack Carson. Primmy had gone to Bognor.

I was pulled out at a great pace through the green and pleasant land. The leisurely sun was going down the sky and *hundreds* of cottontails were frisking in the dark green fields. From a corner seat I was saying goodbye to England, as one ends (or breaks) a love-affair—with appreciation, memory, gratitude.

J writing from St. Leonard's—he wants "our day in the country." Yes.

I had my hair done. See—"a day in the country" . . . which touches a high-water mark in days. I am a little afraid of saying anything about it at all. Memories are so easily murdered. Who wants butterflies mounted under glass?

Feeling adventurous if not dashing I caught, after various alarms and excursions, the 10.25 from Charing X. J was waiting for me at Tunbridge Wells Central, and it was raining. Through the rain I could see that he had become the other one again. Grim-lipped and -eyed. In a friendly, sleepy, frowsty pub we had a drink, and then (it was still raining), caught a bouncing country bus for Mayfield. The country that rolled away to the sky through the rain-dimmed windows of the bus was lovely —*so* green—so rich a land.

Mayfield is three churches, half a dozen shops, an inn of most excellent character, steep brick street and tiny little low-browed cottages—and away from it country lanes and rolling fields.

We had bread and cheese and beer in the pub part of

23

the inn, and grew contenter and contenter for all the rain. J relaxed and became mine again. The innkeeper looked on us with a friendly eye, and offered me a Burberry. We set off down the steep little street and the rain drove us into the church.

We walked round softly, just murmuring. The little church was old and evidently today thriving. It had the atmosphere of a place where people came and lived.

"There's no-one in this church but us," said J softly.

Then Primmy approvingly inspected the Children's Corner and we paced slowly down the nave toward the altar, while I hummed the cliché Mendelssohn wedding march. We lingered for a time, savouring the utter peace.

Then an uncertain sun broke out, and we tramped joyfully abroad.

The green and dripping countryside was good to us. Lanes, overgrown hedges, cart tracks, bunnies, big vine-covered trees, wet moss and "views." Views that rolled away limitless in their generosity.

J was happy. Happy as a sandboy. (He had told his sister about me—I don't know what to think about that. Anyway it's done now.) We both shed all the "buts" that form the very road we walk together, and found a house from which the "view" was demoralizing. I remembered winter, but it was a great effort.

The house was vacant. We sat a long while in the pleasant garden, half-seriously making up stories of the wonderful life we should have there—"if and when."

It must have been four to five miles we did, absurdly at one with this prickly universe. It seemed a good world. Oh, and that inn! Middle House. It *is* old, and heavily beamed and low-ceilinged; *but* that is not all. . . . . Three armchairs were drawn up before great roaring fires. The absolute bliss of dropping my tired body in its great soft Burberry into that chair and feeling the warmth of the coals! J watched me, smiling. After a bit he got up, looked round, bent down and kissed me quickly. He said I looked grand "lying there like some lovely cat stretched out to the warmth."

An hour or so, there. Then an hour or so strolling round again in the rain-washed country and the late sun. On a bench on the road we sat, peace with us.

It was one of those circular seats built around an ancient tree which grew in the middle of the road. We belonged to each other.

That inn where they were so nice to us we left at last and the bus bumped and bounded us on the first stage back to the land of Fact.

I had promised myself that we should stay on and be together for the night in that pleasant place. Alas, as Primmy afterward confessed to her journal:

You know, but for—(a physical condition) we'd have stayed—would we? the night at Middle House.

"Would we?" I knew very well and sympathized with the moral compulsion which imposed that uncertainty and abstention. Like Primmy I had been deeply imbued with the same strict, puritanical code of proper premarital behaviour. And though, like her, in theory I was all for the revolutionary release of Companionate Marriage, in practice upbringing and inculcation were still insistently and effectively forbidding.

25

During the week following that red-letter day at Mayfield we had not managed to meet. I was covering the Beckenham, and then the Queen's Club tournaments—and the trouble at the studio was nearing the point at which it was no longer to be endured. Primmy was aware of it and distressed by it.

Do I, next Saturday, sail or stay here, risking J going *mad* with this cracked melodrama? He should have rung me up this morning. Every time he doesn't I wonder if Jimmy has gone stark, staring mad and pulled a gun on him. Or tied him up and started (with gun) for here. But common sense, of which I still retain a little, assures me that nothing so fictional has happened.

Indeed the danger lay not in overt violence of that kind, but in the heart-searing violence of bursts of unbridled rage, of hurling bitter taunts, sneering, jeering. "You're the world's worst broadcaster." Alternating with sad subsidence into abject apology and pleas. "Let bygones be bygones. Let's make a new start." A pathetic, recurring pattern, recurring and recurring.

From it all Primmy was preparing to escape.

An exceedingly busy day in the City. The Bank, Leadenhall Street. . . . It is never any fag for me to go into the City. At Leadenhall Street and Victoria Street and Trafalgar Square I weighed freighters; and then went for more elaborate information to Messrs. Thomas Cook. Booked on the *Empress*, provisionally. Forgot to mention that I'd had wire from J in AM saying nothing doing today. Then a phone message from Beckenham . . . We agreed that Beckenham was little use to us.

After the Beckenham tournament came the week at

Queen's Club, Baron's Court, runner-up and warmer-up before the Wimbledon fortnight. I took a mid-week respite from my duties, little knowing what was to engulf me at the day's end. But meanwhile, Primmy:

I met J this afternoon at Sloane Square, and we spent the best of two hours sitting in the gardens of the Chelsea Pensioners, with Wren's finest work unregarded by us, but beautifully proportioned nevertheless spread out behind us. It looked gracious and perfect, and the mossy green of the swept lawns added a pensiveness. The nursemaids old and young, or young and unappealing, and their self-engrossed babies, looked neither perfect nor gracious but regrettably of the human race. . . . The afternoon sticks in my mind as a series of babies, prams, dogs, trampled playing-fields, and John's voice. . . .

"I'm very deeply attached to you . . . damn you! Damn you!"

"Did you say 'damn you?' " I asked in considerable surprise.

"I did," said J grimly—but grinned.

As we walked to the bus he said, suddenly gay, "Ach, never mind! We're going to get married some day. Do you know that Primmy?"

"Sometimes," I said.

At the studio, that evening, the inevitable, drearily tiresome sequel to an afternoon of tranquil, pleasant dreaming and renewal was such that I promptly flung a few necessities into a bag and walked out. I had rarely felt so unjustly attacked. I quivered with rage, literally quivered. My limbs shook. Even after the Underground ride from Kensington High Street to Baker Street I had not recovered myself. I hesitated in Dorset Square, half-afraid of the shock to Primmy of my appearing at her door at that hour in that condition. I looked up and saw there was no light in her window. Not in. But perhaps she would be at Moll's room, round the corner in Gloucester Place. I walked about a while before mounting the steps and ringing the bell at No. 3. She was in.

It must have been 10 o'clock or later that there was a knock like thunder on the door and Weaver remarked that "Mr. Coulter would like to speak to Miss Primrose."

I leapt down the stairs, my heart hammering.

J was standing under a green light.

"What is it?" I said half in a whisper.

"It's..." said J, with that queer, desperate grin. "Can you come out darling?"

"Yes," I said rapidly.

"Then get your hat and come. Don't be frightened."

We walked off into the dark street.

"Well," said J. "It's bust up."

"You mean you've left Jimmy?"

"Yes. I've my things in this bag."

We went into Dorset Square to get me a beret.

J took hold of me and looked down into my eyes. "Darling—don't be frightened. I can't have any scared people around. Y'know, it'll be all right."

When we were settled into the top front seat of a bus —and the bus drove on and on through the lights and the night, scattering traffic—"You know you went as white as anything for a moment, there in the hall. I didn't mean to frighten you so. But in case Jimmy writes or telephones or comes round, I had to warn you."

One of Jimmy's ways of trying to harass me had been threats of writing or telephoning Primmy and her friends, telling them offensively what he hoped would embarrass them and me—together with dire warnings that he would

28

be watching in Dorset Square, lying in wait to do **Primmy** and me some undefined dangerous mischief. For it had been part of my policy to give him freely such information as he asked for about where Primmy lived, and the like. I doubted that he would do anything of that kind, for it was not in his normally gentle nature; and I had no reason to think that he ever allowed himself actually to do anything. But that was before what happened on this frightful night. Hence my warning to Primmy.

We descended from the bus at Warren Street station and strode off with very long defiant strides. The Marylebone Road looked very long and broad and intimidating. The buildings colossal, the lighting blinding bright but unable to cope with such a scale.

Whimperingly I said to J, with a half-run to keep level with those grim strides:

"I feel just as if we'd been evicted for not paying the rent."

"Would you stick that?" said J with a sidelong look.

"What?"

"Being evicted for not paying the rent."

"Oh!" said I, with a sort of desperate calm. And the immense street stared at me with its hard blinding night eye. "I don't think I'd mind—all *that*."

I had been teasing her about the sort of harsh life she might well have to face through marrying me. She was about to have a foretaste of it.

In a sordid, unfriendly, melancholy neighbourhood, a wide back street, we tramped into the Raglan Hotel. As J inquired at the desk I looked about. This is life, and so it's a nightmare, I thought. If it was on the stage you'd say, "What a *marvellous* set!" But it's happening. I'm standing on this red plush carpet looking at those red velvet-cushioned settees and chairs. The imitation oak mantel is real. So is the fly-specked mirror, the dusty potted palms, the spittoons, the decaying gentlemen sitting without purpose beside a spindle-legged table for drinks. That woman with the rich, dull black hair and slightly "gone" face is really talking to poor J *about* a 22/6 "room." And the slatternly gentleman in braces and shiny ill-fitting trousers with a shifty Irish face is the "night porter" of this incredible but all-too-existent establishment.

We—and the porter—inspected three slits: a window looking out on the back of the Royal Hotel; a basin; a brass-poster bed; an unsteady "wardrobe," a chair, a piece of worn carpet on which these and the gimcrack chest of drawers reposed.

That dismal seedy "slit" was to serve me as bedroom and writing-room—my "London address"—during the twelve desolate months which followed and when I was not in Ireland. I could afford no better. But it was in Bedford Place, by Bedford Square and the British Museum, in the Reading Room of which I was to spend most of each day—not by morning so sordid a neighbourhood as it had appeared to Primmy on that glum night.

Thankfully at last we tramped out of that bad dream. London, beginning the night, received us with more tenderness. Yes, I told J, I was ready for the night. His step was light from that minute. And his eyes shining. The whole night then was our playground.

We got on a bus and went jolting down. The theatres were just emptying and the lights, the lights, went flaming up into the dark sky.

We got out at Westminster and walked across the

30

Horse Guards Parade, a favourite walk of J's apparently. He likes the space, the darkness of the park on the left and those buildings, carelessly perfect.

People sleeping in the Palace road. Horrible those shapeless, quiet figures lying as still as heaps of old clothes. . . . And the cars roar past them, lights searching the road, the engine—all out. Lords of Creation with the night wind in their hair behind the omnipotent wheel.

It upset J. . . . We hung over the bridge of the Park. Waterfowl dived, swam busily, clucked softly on the dark water. Then we walked up Birdcage Walk and sat on two green chairs outside the barracks, J very exultant.

The area had indeed been a favoured haunt of mine. I had gone there to be alone, thinking out the problems of whatever I was writing, savouring the traditions of the place, the long, low, ancient grey buildings of Whitehall, the broad tree-lined Mall, the silent backs of the great mansions of Carlton House Terrace, the Palace, the Park, and most of all the wide, flat, deserted Horse Guards. And here now was Primmy walking beside me, heightening the happiness of it all.

I fortified my now-sleepy brain, having long drinks of strong coffee in the glare of the blaring Corner House [Lyons in Coventry Street]. We walked across Piccadilly Circus, up Regent Street, across Oxford Circus, past the BBC to our own special route. And now the park, deserted—night here, all right.

Was it two o'clock? Something of that sort.

Over our own little bridge to sit on two green chairs and look at the sleeping roof of Bedford College stables. No-one but the stars, and they were paling anyway to see us!

It was another of those all-night vigils which I have already described, but for me the most needed, most intense.

Before we came back we walked all round the Inner Circle. The stars went out, and that cold, unearthly light came in the sky.

J was happy. He was safe from the megrims with me. Dawn was really in the sky when he left me. I crawled in my stocking feet up the stairs and fell with a soundless groan half sleeping on to the bed.

We were to meet next morning.

By odd coincidence—but doesn't there seem to be an oddness about all coincidence?—just as Primmy was about to leave me and go back to Canada, the BBC asked me to write for them a feature program for short-wave transmission to Canada. The occasion was the tercentenary celebration of the founding of Quebec. It involved work at the British Museum. Waiting at the desk for me in the Reading Room was the book of a Quebec pageant by one of the Lascelles family. I had asked Primmy to come along and help. This she did from time to time—but what was afoot between us was not conducive to the required kind of continuous, single-minded study. Our minds, and our feet, *would* wander.

The morning was coldish and rain falling. I got under weigh early however, and met J outside Warren Street station at 10.30. He looked very *tranquille*, albeit unshaved.

We found ourselves sitting outside the British Museum flanked by those vast pillars, and with the odd Egyptian effigy, a misfit, a cast-out, staring fixedly over our heads. Pigeons hopped about, fouling the long steps. The rain dripped in the great courtyard. J relapsed into hopelessness, and various intellectual lights with an acolyte or so paced up and down across our path.

We had lunch in that nice fruit place in Tottenham Court Road [Shearn's]. We then, hounded by the rain, dived into a News Theatre, a rather stuffy little hall of darkness with an antiquated screen. How much of it J, stretched out motionless in his seat, followed, I could not say.

It was getting on to four when we went back to the hotel for his raincoat.

"Will the lady stay in the lounge, please," said the porter, hurrying after us.

"What!" said J menacingly, halting.

"Will . . ."

"We'll leave the door open," said J and went on.

I dropped onto his bed, thinking this is really very horrid when it happens. Let it remain with Tessa and the Constant Nymph!

J shaved, his mind half on that and half on me. Again, with deep thankfulness, we emerged from the R. H. Dorset Square struck me as haven-like.

Worn out, J dropped on my bed and shut his eyes. I got tea. M telephoned, and I agreed, fuming and frightened, to walk on in *Hamlet*.

My "stage fright" amused J. "You're a funny kid," he remarked, grinning from the bed.

This *Hamlet* was a production at the Steinway Hall in Baker Street by G. W. Knight—who actually cast himself for the role and did play Hamlet. Primmy had known him as a professor in the English Department at Toronto University, and I had known him through correspondence when Middleton Murry was encouraging him to write critical notes on Shakespeare for the Contributors Club of *The New Adelphi*. In that capacity as literary critic he was to gain

33

renown.

I fell asleep. In three-quarters of an hour J woke me. We went out pretty soon. We left his bag at the R. H.

I had gone to the studio to get that bag and more of the things I needed, and fearing another fearful scene had been relieved to find that Jimmy was not in. But I was without a key. The studio was on the ground floor, with a flight of stairs from the centre hall to the studios on the upper floors. I sat down on the stairs to consider how I might break in. From the window on the first landing I saw that a slated roof stretched to a point close to the top of the open window of the studio bedroom—close enough to warrant an attempt to get my legs over the top of that window and then—if I did not come a cropper in the hazardous attempt—I should be able to drop down into the bedroom, collect my things, and leave without Jimmy being aware that I had been in. I crawled across the roof and, lying on it on my back with a grip on the rain-trough, did manage by some gymnastic miracle to get the calves of my legs over the top of the window and then to pull my body after them. I stood in the bedroom in a state of partial shock, wondering how I had managed it, how there had not been a shattering of glass, window-panes smashed in a fearful accident, fearful crash —blood and broken bones in the little courtyard outside the window.

We left his bag at the R. H. and went *via* the British Museum and the student-infested streets of Bloomsbury to . . . a little gay restaurant in Charlotte Street. . . .

It was Vianini's, where luncheon meetings and dinner meetings of *The New Adelphi* had been frequently held while I was still actively with the magazine, meetings at which Primmy had been present.

Tiny tables, mirrors, lights and bunches of white peonies and flame-coloured poppies—and Italian waitresses, loose-hipped, supple-waisted with magnolia skins and careless shrugging shoulders.
It was 10 before we left the little place and walked home to Dorset Square.

She read me the first two chapters of a novel she was writing, *Data for a Life*, and told me of the novel she had completed before leaving Canada, *Household Accounts*. It had just missed winning a much-coveted and famous prize, having reached the final two or three in the *Atlantic Monthly* competition. It was now being read by E. V. Lucas for his firm, Methuen's. I had read it and, with a few minor reservations concerning the introduction toward the end of characters from a class of which Primmy knew little, thought it a sprightly, well-written comedy about the fatuities of the well-to-do leisured people whom Primmy knew well. But I knew of a lengthy account which she had written about her experiences during the grind of three years training as a nurse in a Montreal hospital, the Royal Victoria. It had an immediate reality and vitality, alive with the poignancy and humour of a sympathetic but quick-witted observer.

He wants me to leave it [*Data for a Life*] and go adventuring into the hospital life which he says *means* something. . . .
That being over we consoled ourselves the way the lovers of all time *have*. A monotonous, repetitive ecstasy.

We were soon to have yet another of those midnight wanderings which appealed to Primmy's sense of the romantic and adventurous and in which I found solace.

We jumped a bus to the melancholy Waterloo Bridge. It thundered through the Strand.

The Embankment was gradually falling into desertion. Leaning over and watching the coloured lights, cascades and rivers in the dark water, we saw a police boat shoot out silently on the broad stream. Behind us, trees in full leaf—dark paving stones—brightly lighted cars that rang as they jingled on. The bridge. The far bank in darkness. The sleeping bulk of some derelict ship settling into the water.

We went on. There was the face of Big Ben and twelve striking.

The Horse Guards Parade again; and again because of those sleepers—or those who like Cawdor have "murdered sleep" and therefore "sleep no more"—struck up, up Shaftesbury Avenue (J is betraying an uncharacteristic and as I well know a wholly superficial absorption in clothes. It's all so—heart-breaking.)

We went into the other Corner House, Tottenham Court Road. The orchestra was rather fun, though we were right beside the drums. J was delighting in my summer clothes.

"I know by the women's eyes," he said. "Oh Primmy, it was nice of you to give the English bourgeoisie a treat. Are they playing this queer Spanish thing for you?"

Perhaps the explanation was the garment Primmy was wearing; unusual and decorative—an exotic-looking knee-length light summer coat of loose-woven biscuit-coloured wool, embroidered on breast and sleeves. Her "Indian coat," some called it. Probably it was Californian, but might well have caught the conductor's eye who thought, "Ah! Spanish!" and in compliment struck up accordingly.

"You do, tonight," said J, "look beautiful—not only to my infatuated eyes, either. I've never been able to care —very much—for anyone who wasn't physically attractive."

We walked past the BBC, into Regent's Park, dark at that hour, after 2 AM. Our bridge. Our sleeping pointed stable roof. Our little green chairs.

I had agreed to two nights at Mayfield, there on the embankment in the lights. In the Park, shielded by the green darkness, I went back on it. J was patient, gentle.

"Oh, of course I'd adore it," he said, "but I can do very well without it."

He tried to reason off the fact that I said I was "frightened."

But then he is in love with me.

Dawn was coming up again when we separated. When I turned out my light it showed a roseate glow through the curtain.

Thinking of that conversation I recalled another on a day in April. Primmy confided it to her journal:

I was feeling gay as we walked along in the mild spring sun. I could have capered for the unreasonable joy inside. J grinned. It puzzled, charmed him.

"You've the funniest way of giving a little quick look sideways."

It made me shy for a moment.

We sat over coffee in Lyons's at Great Portland Street. I felt better in the sunlight, walking in the park.

"I am a crassly selfish person," I warned him. "And when I get this thing straightened out, and know what *I* want, I'll make for it, and *you* won't have a chance."

And yet again on a morning in May.

As we went home I said to him, "Remember I'm a backslider and a coward."

"You mean you may want to renege on the whole thing?"

"Yes. Remember what the man said in the poem. 'Holding an ebbing wave.' "

"Yes. Well I've fairly strong hands."

I told him when the time came to make me do what he wanted. He smiled. He doesn't doubt his ability to do that, bless him.

I had sensed from the beginning a hidden dread in Primmy of being irrevocably committed to any kind of alliance. I knew that a sure way of losing her would be to let her think of going on with me as the stealthy fastening of a chain-and-ball on her ankle. Consequently I took care to have her know that whatever might develop between us I should never try nor wish to hold her against her desire. In fact I was to discover to my slightly incredulous surprise and amusement that, even on a day just before we married she reminded me of this assurance, and confirmation of it was a wholly serious but whispered condition of the marriage.

In the production of *Hamlet* by G. Wilson Knight, Primmy was to walk on as one of the ladies-in-waiting. Molly Jones too, was to help, playing some minor roles. Rehearsals were in progress during the first week of the Wimbledon tournament, but I took time to rush round for occasional glances at what was going on between visits to Wimbledon and broadcasts at the BBC. Primmy's journal evokes something of the frenzy of the slightly ridiculous occasion:

Moll had persuaded the little man [Knight] to hold a "crowd" rehearsal at 11.30. It was held about 12.30.

Meantime J looked in and we sat in the extreme back of the half-lighted theatre, chatting.

The stage manager was an old hand, Ben Greet four years. Very funny—father, gran'father too. M fuming. Arrived theatre in a state of deadly calm at 7.

The little dressing-room. Already crowded with somewhat tense-lipped Queen and Ophelia. Bunny [McArdle, an experienced actress and very dear friend of Primmy] makes me up. Like somebody winding up a mechanical toy till the spring is tighter, tighter coiled upon itself.

At last—"The principals!" And, we—as among those horses that do not run—ready.

Overture and "Beginners please!"

Crowding the stairs, our heavy robes and floating veils meeting doublets and clanking mail, cloaks various, beards varied, hose and boots and leggings—a subdued but fervent murmuring:

"Well—good luck!" "Good luck!" "Best of luck!"

Anxious faces, strange in their grease paint. That deadly calm. Hush. From the stage, voices.

We're off!

I have a horror of my entrance—in procession. Into those lights . . . lights, merciless and malignant. I know I *did* curtsey. I know I swallowed in fright, and how I rallied to myself like a mother to its child.

There . . . we've got to get to that line of fire that separates us from the pit. But beyond that curtain is the safe and comfortable dark of the congested wings. There's the S. M., stout, shapeless, amiable, and the dear little boys that play with drums and trumpets and wind-machines. This charitable dimness will receive us. It is the anteroom to complete freedom—the dressing-room, stone steps, little courtyard—off stage.

In that little courtyard by the stage door I found Primmy,

39

looking, in her lady-in-waiting costume, an elegant and lovely lady indeed.

Next entrance. Surely you feel better now?
"Well, yes."
Moll and I are "chatting" with glassy insincerity.
There. That terrible Guildenstern—and in a second the Queen will beckon to M and wave me off.
She's forgotten to wave me off. Never mind, I go.
Follows a long, long period in the wings, the courtyard.
J met us—came toward us as we sought the air. He was amused at me in my clothes.
How peaceful the night sky above us, as in those strange garments we sat, hearing the odd cry from the stage, chatting softly.
I felt pleased with this visible means of support, appearing striding out of the half-light.
Third entrance.
I grin at pink Rosencrantz and dreadful Guildenstern. The Player-Queen makes last unutterable, "Sleep rock thy brain...." The King ... cries for light.
Exeunt—like stampeded sheep.
Ah, the graveyard scene—this isn't so bad. "Hold off the earth awhile, and let me clasp her once more in my arms...." That very noble youth turned out to be an unconscionable bore....
For the last act I did a grand thing. I was late ... wandered on stage, goaded by strong-minded S.M. about five minutes after the curtain had gone up!
The scene begins for me—in this *Hamlet*—when, "Young Fortinbras in conquest come from Poland...." Not that *he* was any hot potatoes—but who can hurt such words?
"Let four captains bear Hamlet like a soldier to the

stage—for he was likely, had he been put on to have proved most royally...."

"The soldiers music and the rites of war ..."

"Go, bid the soldiers shoot!"

Standing on the stage I was covered by this glorious end. The drums, the clear trumpet, the single thunder. Three notes off stage—and those slender bodies, dead.

In the morning, before going to Southfields for Wimbledon, I was happy in taking Primmy's mind off the excitements and miseries of those singular performances.

J and I had a glorious little interlude in the park—Och the day! We lay on the grass worshipping. "I worship this heat."

We saw sails on the river—and swans with steely dove-grey babies sailing like down beside them—and goslings —ducklings with their mamas sailing under the bridge, in and out of the long water weeds....

The matinée! How could I forget it! Sybil Thorndike in front. Unbelievable fag and sweat. Those clothes! Oh *Ham*let!

I was *nearly* late for the last scene again, and everyone was getting twisted in their lines. But somehow it was done. The stage was strewn with dead.

I met the little man's [Knight's] mama.

In a spirit of sleep-walking exhaustion, in silence, we took off our make-up, packed our clothes, trailed out into the kindly night. Only Hamlet was sprinting about like a lad.

In those weeks before she would "sail away" Primmy swung about between contradictory moods and impulses. There was delight at the prospect of so soon being back in Canada with her family and at her beloved island Dah-

wamah; regret and anxiety at leaving me for an uncertain
length of time, possibly to return in the autumn but also—
who could tell?—possibly not to return at all, with some
consequent anxiety about the effect on me of a prolonged absence. "Perhaps some other woman?" A question she confided to her journal but smothered by reminding herself,
"But we put the iron bands round our hearts," and that I
had said I should never marry anyone else. To her journal
she also confided an anxiety which she concealed from me:
even before our grand day at Mayfield she had "struck up a
pleuritic constriction in my right side which was quite
severe . . . spat up two *very* faint traces of blood. Must have
been blood, *je pense*, but perhaps and prob. means nowt."
But that it meant nowt was not confirmed when, later, she
found that "I can't take a long breath yet, but I get caught
on the right side . . . quite a stiff (stiff's the word) attack."
From her hospital training and from the ordeal she had
formerly endured as a patient in a sanatorium for TB, she
knew the dire threat; but with that optimism which seems
to sustain TB patients, she brushed it aside. She counted her
money and, with what she had in excess of the minimum
required to sail, she spent and enjoyed spending: having
her hair done expensively and, she said, ruined in Bond
Street; having it done again *"pour le moment*—too 18th
century, delicious—alas, soon to be destroyed by—ardour"*;
seeing and buying a "poem of a hat—10 bob too—as useless
and impracticable as a poem"; shopping in Lilywhite's and
Lafayette's.

The sun—the streets—the shops—the crowd—oh my
London!
At Lilywhite's, as I had two pounds to the end of the
month, I chose a lovely pair of navy slacks, a pair of navy
rope sandals and—thrown in—a silk striped shirt in blue.
At Lafayette's I paused to select a parrot-yellow bathing-

suit and cap, and wide coarse yellow straw with shallow
navy ribbon crown and scarlet under the brim.
Snack lunch *chez moi*.

But why not? She reminds herself of my remark—made
in a different context:

"Oh Primmy, we'll soon be under the sod like all the
others before us. Are we not to *take* it when life flames up
for a moment into something beautiful?"

When E. V. Lucas had read her novel *Household Accounts* Primmy was called to see him at Methuen's. She and
I met in the park, and in an enchantment of sun and the
scent of flowers walked down that long straight drive from
the Zoo to Marylebone Road.

The cultivated borders, on this morning tenderly
blooming in a thousand colours. They almost sang, those
things that glowed and nodded in the light morning
breeze. I parted from J, and he went to the Museum and
I to Essex Street.
E. V. Lucas: (Advancing to meet me. In that fatherly
well-lived tone:) How nice you look!
Me: . . . .
E. V. L.: Much better without a hat!
Me: I . . . I shall be sailing in ten days.
E. V. L.: But you haven't had the proofs yet, have you?
Me: . . . . ?
E.V.L.: Aren't we bringing out a book of yours? Let me
see—it was about a fireman, wasn't it?
I gently put him right.
"Oh but I remember. That book. I remember I liked
it extremely well. It's a *much* better book than the one I
was thinking of. But it could wait a bit, quite well."

Lucas had himself had his great success with a novel written in the same manner as was Primmy's—in which all comes to light through a series of letters—letters in which the characters write about each other. So he knew the difficulties, and praised Primmy, saying that the letters her characters wrote had the feel of real letters, unlike those of most authors who attempt a novel in that manner. But he thought it a rather special type of novel, not the best in which to introduce a new writer. He asked her to be patient, lay it aside for the present, write another, of the ordinary conventional kind, and this he would publish. Having, through it, gained a hearing for Olive Clare Primrose, he would bring out *Household Accounts*.

"I mean to do all that. Certainly. Now you're going back to Canada. And you're going to write to me, and keep in touch with me. And you'll write that other novel."

Somewhere in this conversation he told me I could consider that they had accepted H.A.

We parted. E. V. saying with genial appreciation, "You do look nice!"

To take back to Canada as the spoils of her foray into literary London, this provisional acceptance was not what Primmy needed. In the year to come she might write that other novel, but she, and I, wanted an unconditional acceptance for publication now. So she was pleased when I thought of showing *Household Accounts* to Helen Waddell whose work we both admired and whom I knew through my work at *The New Adelphi* and through my acquaintance with her brother Sam (Rutherford Mayne) perhaps the best of the playwrights and actors of the Ulster Literary Theatre. Helen Waddell welcomed the novel as "just my sort of thing," and proposed offering it to Constable's, for whom she worked.

If the response of a publisher to submission of a first novel by an unknown writer be that of Lucas—first write another of a more popular kind—I knew it might well be no more than a much-used publishers' device to clap a halter on an author regarded as uncertain to win the race this time but worth grooming for another. But for Primmy, merely that Helen Waddell should like the book was in itself an achievement to take with her when she sailed back to Canada. And it was much needed, when in those weeks before her departure the swing of her moods was often toward the shadow side. I had begun to think of it as the dangerous shadow side. Deeply depressed, she would retire into what she called "this refuge, this harbour, this port-in-a-storm."

J of course would see that I was "down the tunnel," as he put it.

I thought I would take my heavy heart out of reach and get what solace I could out of my little room. . . . This scrap of a room, which isn't big enough to pace up and down. I could only lie in bed, crouch on the floor. Because I am alone more than I was [before she ceased to live with Molly] and because I am so unhappy.

The evening is so late and has been drivelled away. It has all gone now my beautiful evening however shining and unused and bright with virtue it looked when I came in, weighed down with a clump of ungainly parcels and oppressed by "Solitude walks on heavy steps more near."

And again, as what she spoke of as The End drew near.

What had I done with this day? It's gone—and a certain evening peace—that descends on the solitary potterer who has successfully turned a deaf ear to duty—bathes me. I have celebrated a few mystic cave-woman beauty

45

rites. And I have lain on my back, bare-legged on the bed, smoking, drinking weak China tea, enjoying the strange mind that carved out "The Notebook" [Rainer Maria Rilke]. I have run, swinging over the hot pavements of the Imperial City in its Sunday mood. I have regained my chair, my China tea, my green-graced open window.

This time next week—where, eh? Well, I think, I do truly think now, "the ocean blue." Five more little days of this—this strange semi-tragic sojourn. So, all day, marching side-by-side with Solitude, went The End. I don't feel—not yet anyway—wildly sad. Only melancholy, distrait.... I think I'm tired.

I was aware of that melancholy. I did what I could to lighten it.

I said good-bye to J last night, nearly in tears. He does not *know* how my head sizzles with the heaped coals of fire when he tells me that I am gentle and generous and how wise I have been. "You've been a gem. I didn't know you had all this in you."

But the swing in mood was also often over, and well over, toward the other side—the gay, spirited, happy and laughing Primmy. It was the second, the final week of Wimbledon. I had the joy of having her with me, watching the matches, watching the people:

Took Inner Circle to Gloucester Road, where I met J. We went down to Wimbledon, a rather happy ride. Wimbledon itself, exciting, and heavenly heat—the sun *beat* down.

J and I had tea in the enclosure. How abominably dressed is the English crowd, I thought with languid superiority. J watches me. Never takes his eyes off me....

46

Then that glorious match on the Centre Court: Van Ryn and Allison against the little Japs. Later, a long bout of standing in the air-exhausted Centre Court. I was too tired for this.

We ambled in the great throng. Sun—glorious. Crowd exciting. J and I utterly isolated, alone in the multitude. I don't know what time we pushed through that crowd of saunterers, and left.

In an ABC—J attacked his notes. I am used to those "marble" tables. They are the symbol of this, which has been rich in one thing only—love.

We had a delicious aspic-cum-salad cum coffee and sweet in the restaurant of the BBC. Very like a film, this. J rather gay, and enjoying demonstrating his pet toy.

Then we went up to a listening-room which, mercifully, was empty. J's stuff not his first-flight. He himself disgusted with it—called it "a flop, a washout, bloody."

But she had been in the listening-room on other evenings, and had been, she told me, proud, finding what I had to say about these, the world's greatest players, enlightening, "first-rate criticism" and recalling descriptive phrases such as "the ball stiff with spin." I had told her what fascinated me about offering criticism of these players—who if permitted by an opponent could hit a ball to any precise point they pleased on the court—was the searching manner in which they first assessed the stroke-play and the form of an opponent, and adopted a strategy accordingly; and then, most fascinating of all, my own assessment of the psychological endowment of a player, and how it affected his performance. Good criticism of these matches had for me, something of the quality of a challenging book review.

The snapshots we took at Wimbledon were among the best we had of each other, and were added to those we had taken in "our field" in Regent's Park. A mishap with these had given Primmy a distressing jolt.

J inspected the snaps. One *glorious* one of him; one belligerent Irish one; one worried but rather sweet. One of me with make-up mirror, a bit Laura Knight; and one engaging one, bundled in that kind gent's Burberry smiling into the wind, at Mayfield.

Why these details? Only that this afternoon on an 11 bus, or in the Army and Navy Stores, or between Charing Cross and the Stores, I lost the lot. Yes! So, was I speechless!

I made inquiries, and next day as we walked through the park I had a surprise waiting for her.

We walked with the lime throwing its cool scent on the air, to Baker Street. In that limbo of absent-mindedness [the lost-and-found office] my blessed snaps were restored to me.

During the long separation which was about to engulf us, we should have these reminders of days together—but in addition we each went to the theatrical photographers, Reprograph, and sat for several "cabinet" photographs. Babs' incredulous comment on one of her:

Saw strange film-star photo of me—Dolores del Rio —one of us, anyway.

I met J and we had a session in "our field"—chewing grass, glorifying the sun-god, Apollo, ruminating, J with anxiety and I with a forerunner of contrition—she loves him, she-loves-him-*not*...!

(Tell me, am I really in love? Thing is he's *vital*, that man, that stranger. He's alive and strides like a giant, sometimes. Anyway, it makes me happy—like someone has lit a glorious, generous fire—just for *you*.)

Babies and dogs, dogs and babies; swans, and fluff of silver; ducks, and fluff of gold. I suddenly realized the incredible, today: time is marching on, and I am going. Three—I said three—days separate me from it. I suppose I have been trying not to take it in.

"I who am really a believer in miracles, would not be too surprised if some craft brought you (J) to land." Written, thinking of Dahwamah, and nowhere in its singing woods, John.

I am in bed, that spot of spots. . . . I see that I shall be terribly lonely . . . I'll feel naked, vulnerable as a baby when I'm alone again.

I, too, saw that I should be terribly lonely. The last stage of that gradual disentangling from Jimmy had arrived. For many weeks my presence in the studio had been intermittent. Stage by stage he was being brought to see that our long span of mutual sharing and companionship was indeed about to end. The moment was appropriate. For it had long been our custom to leave London—as formerly to leave Dublin—at the end of June to go back to spend the summer each with his own family in Belfast. This was the point that I had decided—since his bitter, half-insane hostility to change meant that there could be no possibility whatever of the civilized acceptance I at first had hoped for—should be that end. I should never again be part of the life of that studio; now associated with so many violently unhappy and sad scenes, but formerly a place that I had loved, for as a place to live in London it had many attractions. It was one of a set of studios on the south side of Edwardes Square, near Holland House, South Kensington. It was, I believe, London's second largest square, second only to Lincoln's Inn Fields. It overlooked the grass tennis court, on which Jimmy and I had often played, in the very pleasant gardens

—gardens into which the people who lived in the charming little houses which surrounded the Square—houses built for the accommodation of Huguenot fugitives from France —used on warm summer evenings to come out after dinner in their evening clothes, cross into the gardens and wander about, idly chattering and laughing, the ladies in their long dresses, a scene elegant as one of those delicate fancies, *fêtes champêtres*, of Watteau.

I had loved the enormous studio-room, with its window filling the entire north wall and its balcony at the back like the music-gallery of some mediaeval banqueting hall. Alas, after a few days I should not be there ever again.

Jimmy asked me to meet him at the Majestic, a restaurant then just opened in Kensington High Street by, as I was told, two American women with a repertoire of dishes, sandwiches and ice creams of kinds hitherto unheard-of in London. We met. He was quiet, distressed, had little to say beyond that he was going home that evening, back to Belfast. We parted, he to pack his belongings, I to Wimbledon and then to join Primmy who also was packing, for it was the eve of her departure. I found her in her little room, distraught by the sight of her baggage, more of it than I had ever seen in use by any one person.

That unbelievable welter of uprooted things. The mass formation of suitcases, the bed sinking under its load of unpacked, unrelated objects. And John, in his shirt-sleeves, with the grin never entirely gone, writing labels, tying brown paper parcels with string, chivvying, arguing, condemning—and adoring his distraught love!

He laughed suddenly, looking up from the string. "You know, things that would irritate me past bearing in anybody else, in you—how did you *think* you were going to do it, darling?"

I collapsed against him; in that absurd tangle of absurd possessions—they faded in all their unpackable ranks—the little room revolved once or twice and then simply went out like a candle. . . .

At last J sat down, and pulled me down, utterly exhausted.

"Would you like to sleep a bit?" he whispered.

"No—no! Oh darling, I *must* do it."

About 1.30 he peered out of the open window, I turned out the light so he could see better. It was a strange moment, standing there blind, with the night outside.

We went out, as quiet as thieves, and into the unnoticing night. We walked along to the coffee-stall near Edgware Road. We had a little much-needed sustenance. Ah, how delicious it was!

Then at a great pace I set out with him, and we strode with the walk of hill-billies as far as Paddington. We didn't say much. It was some comfort just to be together, walking like mad away from the business of packing. He put me into a taxi and I watched him go off into the deserted city. Then, half-sleeping, I clung to the slippery leather seat. When I got to Dorset Square I thought very brilliantly how to pack the unpackable.

Fell asleep, wakened by a mouse, at 6.15.

I walked on, through Bayswater and Kensington to the studio, rarely meeting anyone, seeing an occasional policeman on his beat going from house to house with his flashlight trying the doors. It was half past two. Jimmy had gone. I sat down in the dark and silence, sad, thinking of all that had happened there; then turned in and slept, but was up again by seven next morning. I went at once to Dorset Square, and as I turned into it from Balcombe Street saw Primmy, already abroad, coming round from Moll's.

It was here, the parting. I met John, as I was returning

from a fruitless attack at Moll's door. It was funny, standing there at 8.10 on the corner. All blurred, this bit. A moment when we gazed around on our handiwork in the little dismantled room. J gave me one last hurried kiss where we had had so many unhurried. Then, the last things to go down. The taxi.

It was a relief to be sitting there, leaning against J. All finished. All over. Oblivious of the faces passing by. Selfridge's. Hyde Park. "Madam, when will you see Hyde Park again?" I don't know. It is the silent panorama background.

The taxi turned clumsily through the gates. Constitution Hill. The Palace. The memorial, glittering, sunwashed. Birdcage Walk.

"We sat *there*, do you remember?" John was holding me.

"Well," I said. "Hold on to me."

"What?"

"Don't lose me."

"No," said John, and he laughed, not very successfully. Still, a laugh. "I've been too long finding you to lose you now."

"Oh darling," said John. "Waterloo. We're here." His voice was sad.

I should have liked to go with her, on the boat-train to Southampton. But it was Saturday, the last day at Wimbledon, and I had undertaken to be there for the finals of the women's singles, Moody vs. Round. Primmy and I walked to-and-fro, to-and-fro on the platform, arm-in-arm, simulating a gaiety of mood though sick at heart. We saw some of the players in that *Hamlet*, including the Canadian who had played the Queen. "Dreadful to have to recognize anyone *now*," said Primmy. We agreed that, however desolating this parting, it was in all the complex circumstances,

52

right. "To agree that a thing is 'right,' " said Primmy. "There is something incredibly pathetic about it, isn't there. It's the very password of defeat." I got a platform ticket, and we found the carriage in which Primmy was to travel.

I felt utterly near him. I felt we were one being, and only our physical form, two phantoms, were being torn apart.

"Take your seats please!"

Obediently I broke away toward the train. But John, who had been debating whether to kiss me here and be damned to them, suddenly held me and turned my face to his. He kissed my mouth, not hurriedly, only with an intensity as if to keep us both going till this should pass.

Then the train. Wave—yes, and throw him all the kisses you like. See—so will he! He sketches a comic turn with outstretched hat—lover implores his mistress to smile. Sure, I can smile. Smile and cry.

And he was gone.

The last I saw of her was her hand and arm waving to me as the train curved away out of the station. I was left in a daze of desolation, dry-eyed but near to tears, suffering as one suffers in the first anguish of bereavement. I sent a *bon voyage* telegram to the ship, and was, that evening, to get one from it, love and farewell. Luckily I had to go on about my business: Wimbledon, and then for the next few days, settling bills, stewing in the Reading Room of the British Museum in preparation for new programs I had undertaken, and for the Quebec tercentenary salute to Canada; and finally, the clearing up and closing of the studio. In this I left behind all my books and some of my clothes—books, many of them first editions—including a set of Middleton Murry's inscribed to me—as were many from authors with whom I had dealt during my time at *The New Adelphi*. I knew that if I did not remove them now I probably never should—and at that disconsolate moment, caring little about them or anything else but the emptiness and misery of existence in Primmy's absence, I abandoned them—perhaps in half-conscious continuation of my plan to avoid not only the perilous abrupt break with Jimmy, but also the leaving of any evidence that I intended an absolute break eventually.

On the Thursday following that Saturday of farewell to Primmy, I left London and went back to work, and to endure the long separation from Primmy, in Belfast.

2

Before I left the studio I had two letters from Primmy—one posted at Southampton, one at Cherbourg.*

RMS *Empress of Britain*
Saturday, 6 July, 1935

John darling, you'll get this tonight, won't you? *And* another from Cherbourg on Monday.

It's such a picture-postcard of a day—all glittering. . . . That ridiculous label, "Wanted on Voyage"—when one is invariably "wanted" from the fading shore! All my absurd Heath Robinson luggage is with me.

The journey down was very sticky and hot. And this "floating palace" leaves me singularly cold. Anyway the get-away by train is merciful. That gap of widening water

*I shall frequently omit from these letters commonplaces of salutation; and reiterated endearments, fume of the literature of love.

is a harping on the business. I don't feel here at all. I just seem to be on the platform with you.

What happens when one leaves oneself behind? Do you remember the fairytale where the Prince put iron bands round his heart to prevent it from breaking?

RMS *Empress of Britain*
Saturday, 6 July, 5.30 PM

. . . In half an hour we get to Cherbourg, my last chance to talk to you for days and days. I'm trying to hear the broadcast [BBC—my comments on the Wimbledon finals]. But I don't suppose they'll bother to send me where I can hear it. I may think differently by Thursday, but it seems to me a sanguinary boat. The deck space is all winches and hawsers and rods and poles and perches. The dining-room is small. The cabin'll do. As for the *people*—my dear a deputation of the dull by their looks. *Deadly*. There are no amusing, chewing foreigners even—no kids—*no*-one. So long, my darling.

A fortnight was to pass before I heard from her again—a letter written and posted aboard ship.

RMS *Empress of Britain*
Wednesday, 10 July.

John darling, I have disgraced you. *And* proved myself no child of my father. [Dr. Primrose—a good sailor, who relished to elation even the turbulence of the sea.] I have been *so* sick!

I hate this boat. I knew I would. A little more and I'd be a lunatic, that's what. I am practically one now. Yes, between the *shattering* vibration which never lets up—and now takes place entirely inside my head—and the long, slipping roll—and the slight pitching—and the quite staggering amount of noise—machinery grinding, grating, babies yelling, crates banging. . . . I am only a phantom of myself. A cursing phantom, letting out blindly at the wall with my fists, and shouting a little extra blasphemy into the 5 AM racket. I have suffered from the sea before, but never this.

That first night, when I was sitting in the lounge, it seemed impossible to believe it really *had* happened. I kept thinking you'd come through the door, throw that "lowering" look (to which I am so attached!) round the sloppy company, and then cross over to me in four strides. But one of those inspired jingle-strummers went on getting the piano to repeat last year's jazz. What is sadder? The half-circle of faces vaguely came in on the chorus—and the people playing cards went on with an interminable blurred conversation. And on deck a cold wind blew out of a pale cold sky. And you—oh darling how I am missing you!

Only one day, and that was Sunday morning, of hot sun on the top deck. Where were you that Sunday morning?

I am writing in the celestial "First" [She was travelling "Third" but went where she pleased, as was her wont.] with dove-grey carpet under my common feet. I just—*got* here.

We'll land—perhaps tonight. But you'll hear all about it right away. Do you miss me? How much? Oh darling listen—January, be it, but no longer, no longer, I couldn't bear it. Have you written to me? Lots of times? *Have* you? Because I *must* be supported. I love you.

That was the first time I had heard from her those three words. Of the remainder of the voyage she was to tell me in letters, but I find it more freely written in her journal:

At sea. RMS *Empress of Britain*
Well, it's happened. I am going farther and farther from him every minute. And besides, I love him. . . .

On deck a half-gale blows out of the pale sunset. The sea is flat and very cold, and the light of the sky mingles in a common dusk. The ship throbs on her course. The vibration is shattering in the 3rd. . . .

And John is—10.30—in that pub—getting tight—or what? Ah, darling wait a bit—it'll *be* all right.

Ah, it's no good. I'm tired to the very *core*. And nothing is going to occur on this trip. . . . I hope he's all right, this night when I'm going so far away. He smiled, suddenly, a little wryly, at the train.

"What?"

"Only that I wish I wasn't so in love with you when you're going so far away."

It seems to keep him close to me, this. But I'll go breathe the sea, and sleep.

Sunday, 7 July. Second day out.

9.20 AM

I am sitting up on the Tourist top deck. V. pleasant sun. Gloriously hot. I have no business to be here, of course. But I got here by accident and here I stay. I think I'll spend so much time in the Tourist that the very ranks of Tuscany won't know where I belong.

5.40 PM

It's turned cold. The sun has gone. My hands are now too numb to write. And my head aches—anyone would get the megrims with this confounded shuddering, shaking misery. This trip promises to be pretty frightful—but it can't, appearances to the contrary, last forever.

Monday, 8 July.

Made an abortive attempt to have a very late breakfast. Then threw in my hand, retired to bed and spent the day very light of food. I thought a lot. I married J at the Church of St. Bartholomew the Great, among other things. I thought of John persistently. I thought that he was one of the best and most protective souls. I laid my

57

head, which was split in half with pain, on his shoulder. I thought of making this voyage t'other way round in January. I cursed this ship, every time it pitched or rolled or shook. I cursed its food, its crew, and all its works.

Yesterday, by lunchtime, I was up—brandy. I felt restored to boredom—the smell of the lounge, the screaming of the children, the slimy cold of the wet decks.

Wednesday, 10 July.
Fifth day at sea. Fog off Cape Race. Speed very low. Yes, well—that's merciful isn't it? A little more of this *bon voyage* and I should be a lunatic. By tomorrow— *terra firma*, surely. I no longer care . . . if only it is *terra* and *firma*.

Thursday, 11 July. 8 AM
I have just heard the shattering news that we don't dock till 12.30 midnight.

Concert with Indian chief, last night.

After all this trip has brightened considerably. And oh, the St. Lawrence tonight. Those great hills towering up from the sunset-sleeping water! The lovely giant sleeping outline. The sweet breath of the balsam. The first star! I crouched on a hatch, watching the dark rush of the water. The shores were in shadow, and the liner swept on at speed. I went to bed.

Friday, 12 July.
It wasn't difficult to wake up—the last awakening from those shallow slumbers, thin as the bunk that cradles them.

Breakfast was an "awfully jolly" meal. . . . Relieved to think we would soon be irretrievably separated, everyone became surpassingly matey. Even the bleakness of that zero hour was no check to our amiability; even the prospect of pressing a *pourboire* upon the sneering Pooh-bah failed to damp us down.

I have known worse disembarkings. Infinitely longer. More arm-breaking. Why, in a very reasonable fraction of time we were gazing out of the dusty windows of the standing train at the broad stern of the empty *Empress*, heavily, humbly, at peace. Busy little forms toiled back and forth, their laden figures making unsteady grade of the gangway with varying degrees of unsteadiness. She would be going down the river, headed for the open sea that night.

I sat in the humble grit-encrusted quarters reserved for hill-billies, rather disliking their shirt-sleeves, their crumpled curls, their fretful young. I comforted myself by writing to John in a remote, happy, humorous and loving vein. It cut off direct contact.

Quebec. Friday morning.
En Route, CPR

Oh *John*, that cable! [I had sent it to await her arrival at Quebec.] How I blessed you for it! Everyone thought one cocktail had done me a phenomenal amount of good; but the fact was I'd gone into my cabin on the way to dinner and found it. . . . And that telescoped the whole interminable voyage!

We're sitting in the sheds at Quebec. There are sort of cliffs outside. They look very clear and white. It seems unfortunate that here I *am*, and no use to you. [I had asked her to send some particulars for use in the Quebec program on which I was working.] I'm sorry I can't step off and do a little research. But I can't, darling; can't even get you a picture postcard—helpful as I *know* that would be.

I have separated from all the respectable travellers, and am sitting in a car, composed exclusively of hill-billies. The hill-billy is a grand chap on the films. He's a little oppressive in private life—though life is so far from private! And his conversation, particularly in a heat wave, is unbelievably limited.

We're off! Wheels are sublime, aren't they?

There's the harbour, and there's the stern of the old *Empress*, re-loading, poor soul.

Coming up the river last night was lovely. Oh how I wished you'd been there. Some day we'll have to do it, you see? *Have* to. It's so huge, the St. Lawrence; and last night at sunset there was not a ripple and we swept up passing what seemed like toy ships beginning to light up—and those gigantic hills, towering on either side.

We're really off. This is my own, rough, tough, gravelly, weed-grown country. At the ship's concert a Mohawk Indian chief who'd been singing in *Hiawatha*, performed. He had a lovely voice, and the canoe song was something to hear. He had a most impressive head on him, too. The old chap, with his thick black hair hanging in a long bob behind his ears, had a broad, strong, dignified face the colour of copper, and small intelligent eyes, and the manner and bearing of a great man, although he was as squat as a chimp. Then he said he'd light a fire with two sticks and a mouse's nest and have a blaze in 30 seconds. "My people believe fire a mysterious and great thing," he said. And he did it all right. The mouse's nest blazed up nicely in less than half a minute!

The celebrated flyer is picking up speed, and an incredible number of cinders is with us. The white-washed barns and frame houses look small in the enormous untidy fields.

How do you think I managed—me and my eleven cherished "pieces"—to get off that boat—without you, I mean? Were you worrying about me?

I shall be sick, on wheels on the good land, if I persist in writing to you while the train rocks on at this rate. I'll sign off for the minute, John darling   —Primmy.

Friday-Saturday, 12-13 July.
The night on the train was hill-billies all the way.
Very hot—a malign glare of swinging lamps—a rush of
hot, thick air—a crowding of petulant human animals,
humble creatures, a bit smelly thus overcrowded, but
essentially inoffensive.

I shook myself awake at last, when the troubled night
and all its cramped dreams seemed over. The country
flying past took on light, form, substance, shadow. I tried
to jerk myself into a receptive state. I said—look! Look!
You *are* home. Look, it's over! It *is* over! You are *here*
again.

I tried to repair the night's work on my face. Father
was there to meet me.

I too, had arrived home, and for a fortnight had been
busy arranging my work for the coming summer and
autumn. The pleasantest part of it—my summer holiday—
was that here in Ulster, after Wimbledon, I was to continue
at the weekly round of tennis tournaments, now for the
Northern Ireland station of the BBC. These I much enjoyed. There could hardly be a greater, more amusing
contrast than that between the English tournaments and
their formalities, and the Irish, in which a town or county
club invites all comers to compete: as for the public—if they
cared to look in they'd see some fun. At one of these tournaments, as I stood outside the wire-netting enclosure of the
best court, I remember thinking of the Wimbledon Centre
Court with all its proprieties and grandeur, and then suddenly laughing out as I saw, on the other side of the netting,
a donkey on his back in the long grass, rolling and braying
in contented unconcern.

It was Saturday, 21 July. For the finals of men's singles
I was at the tournament at Bangor, a pleasant seaside town
on Belfast Lough. But, rain having stopped play, I sat in the

tent provided by the ladies of the club and was unsociable enough to sit by myself, avoiding the lively conversation and banter, reading. Reading a letter I had received that morning from Primmy. She had by now arrived at Dahwamah.

Dahwamah
Gordon Bay PO
Ontario, Canada

So they came to the place that was once called Paradise.

Wednesday, 17 July.
Father met me himself and he is so polite he never said, what a thing you look, my child! And, oh John, I did indeed. I looked too tough for words. I, with precipitancy, to my hairdresser. The poor man nearly *swooned* when he saw the wild Indian returning from the hub of civilization! He was polite, too, but firm, not to say drastic. I am sorry, darling. You would probably complain if you saw me now. Or would you—*complain?*

Where are you, John? It's beginning to seem an *interminable* time since I heard. You see, there's only one mail a day up here, and on each side of that hour the illimitable desert rolls to the horizon. [By "desert" she means wilderness of lakes and wooded islands.] I am squatting on a rock in the sun, the glorious sun, the woods growing very green and pine-needly all round me, and the blue lake racing past in the wind that blows this letter inside out. What a morning, darling! What a *morning!* If, if, *if*—you could only smell the balsam this morning! The air is quite heavy with balsam and sun. And the primeval forest looks grand—and the deep woods are all shot through with that sun. And as for the lake—some day, *some day* it will be our first morning here, and we'll sit just precisely *here* and *see* this—and on that night by special arrangement with the management there will be a moon.

I am a little crazy because the sun is *so* hot, and to be loose again in my wild woods. It has gone to my head—but strange as it may seem—I miss you. Have you ever had pleurisy? It catches you out when you breathe—well, that's a bit like it. But I've *brought* you here, darling. It's just that I'd like to be able to put out my hand and *touch* you.

Oh, what's the use of talking? *When* do you think I'll get my first letter?

She got it two days later, for I had written it on the day after she sailed, and in the meantime had written three others. The first of these that has survived opened with a dialogue between two people—Primmy and me— in a pretended radio play. It recalled some of our happy times together. Its title was *Episode Over*:

68 Campbell Park Avenue
Strandtown, Belfast
21/7/35

[Following the dialogue] . . . A lovely morning and I'm sentimentally thrusting myself back to *those* lovely mornings! But—it *is* silly. Damn silly! I'll write a play to capitalize on the silliness of it. Or a film. Yes, better a film. Title: *Episode Over*. There'll be shots of various pubs and cafés, tennis at Weybridge—Mayfield—Wimbledon—the BBC—Horse Guards—a jumble of luggage—Waterloo. Desolation.

Let's dodge desolation anyway. . . . I want to, and do, think of you as growing brown and bonnie [she had not told me about that scare—that "slight pleuritic constriction" and spat-up blood, but I had fears for her, a constant unspoken anxiety], stretching out lazy limbs to the sun on your island, away there—and being serene and happy with your people.

You've a right to be very happy after that terrible ocean

crossing. What an ordeal! I've watched every bit of the way as you went on and on, and only now am I beginning to be a bit easier in mind about you, thinking you won't be such a fool as to do anything but get your body brimmed up with health and bonniness.

Of *course* I'll write to you. . . . But there's a terrible lot of stiff, stiff work to be battered through. And I'm at it, Primmy. I'm at it. . . . Trying to get away with that Quebec program, and one other for Canada. Just the first tentative adumbration of an idea that I might, on some of these programs, find a reason to go to your country before the winter. But it's very hard to manage. Very. I shouldn't have whispered it to you, it's so improbable.

There's a Professor Ernest Macmillan of Toronto to whom I've been referred for Canadian music. . . . He's in London, working at the BBC on some musical program —"from old Canada!" I was to meet him, had I remained in London. Do you know him?

Send me more snaps. I'd like a complete snap-record of you and the island and the house and everything about Dahwamah. . . . And aren't there any guide-book sort of things about Muskoka generally? You see—you see—I want to be there by even such vicarious or proxy contacts.

You ask do I miss you, and how much? Can't you guess from this letter that the answer is: yes, yes, yes—and terribly. You say, write, please write. . . . I'll shoot off letters to you like bullets out of a machine-gun—if you'll shoot as many back. Ah, but I longed for that boat-letter of yours . . . and I was touched and uplifted by the last three words of it. Words heard from you for the first time. And I repeat them. "I love you"   —John.

About every third day from that time on each of us was to have a letter from the other. (Every one of these 254 letters has, for me, an interest beyond that which I could suppose they might have for anyone else; so that, even if it were feasible to reproduce them all in full I would not do so here. Indeed I shall have, in general, to confine myself to quoting no more than brief excerpts from a very few.) One result was that Primmy, having written to me of the day's doings, confided less and less of them to her journals; and much of what she did confide concerned her reunion with members of her family and with friends, none of whom was at the time known to me. For these homecoming reunions she went off on jaunts, to and fro between Dahwamah and Toronto, and between Muskoka and the Georgian Bay; jaunts which were also a reunion—reunion with familiar and loved summer scenes in which she looked around her with delight. Her descriptions of them in her letters were part of her series of word-pictures designed to lead me, a stranger to her country, to see it in imagination and long to come to it and know it in reality.

From her seat in the train she sees the youngsters at play along the banks of the river Don:

There is something ridiculous and confident in those jaunty buttocks of the young, red-brown figures, almost nude—but for pale abbreviated trunks, nude—that stood with careless arms and careless tufted hair on the high, sandy banks of the river. The morning sun is theirs; the summer-parched stream, trickling languidly between those heat-crumbled banks is theirs. Their very reckless-ness this morning belongs to them . . . they may be far too young to die (in the risks they take) but at least they have cheated death this morning.

She revisits the Joy family on their island in Nares Inlet, Georgian Bay, having first renewed a thrill of childhood at a "wiener roast."

Dahwamah, Gordon Bay
Wednesday, 21 August.
Nando [Alex Joy] and I, rather late in the evening,
started out by canoe for a bonfire. The sky was stormy and
the waves quarrelsome. When we reached that flare between the rocks, it looked like some pagan ceremonial. For
the night was a black-out, and in that red glare the young
copper-coloured faces and bodies reverted to the Indian!
The presiding genius, nineteen years old, a bouncing aggressive young person, looked, from sheer health and life and
sun-coloured skin, as if she was representing the goddess of
earth. The youngsters had a gramophone on the rocks. I
felt, I may say, 104, sitting in the solicitous dark! Who but
my Nando would wish to take his *aunt* to a bonfire?

I feel as if I had never *really* told you about the Georgian
Bay. A train from Gordon Bay disgorged me and several
other optimists on a small ridge at Pointe-au-Baril, very
high against the sky and overlooking a small neck of water
and a small fleet of little craft. An ancient launch agreed to
take me to "the shop." [The point at which one ventures
out into the reefs of the open water on the way round to
Nares Inlet.] We spent that fine afternoon cruising in the
"tame" part of the bay, I lying out on the so-called deck,
which had no awning, and lapping up the sun, the reeds, the
pines, the reefs, the heavenly blue of sky and water—while
the laconic gent who ran the boat attempted to dispose of a
case of whisky.

Eventually we arrived at the "shop"—a shack, perched
on a shoulder of rock with a little sparse, wind-twisted bush
around it. An amiable collection of students working for
their next year told me the boss was away. In two and a half
hours he would—perhaps—come back. However an enterprising youth salvaged a very old launch and we towed a
boat (for emergencies) and started for the inlet. The "open"
has a roll of Atlantic proportions and a wind always blow-

ing. Inside the reefs are the islands, innumerable and very small. We got here by the Grace of God. . . .

When that enterprising youth landed me from the aged launch at Nina's island, I ran up the path, hallo-ing into the utter desertion. No-one at home. *But* there was Weekes [a Scots terrier]. There *was* that "face among faces" *pressed* against the window screen. Such a welcome to a prodigal! Weekes cried with excitement. She made short whimpering runs round me, and I sat down on the floor and we embraced in a perfect frenzy of reunion! I was glad, and so I told her, that there was no-one to see that scene or to distract us. We sat on a high rock and stared to see at last the canoes string around the point. Mystified canoes, quite unable to distinguish *who* was sitting like Buddha on the rock, clasping their knees. And first Howard [Joy—Alex's younger brother] fell out of the canoe with a choked, "Oh Babs!" [Primmy's name in the family]. Then Nancy [Joy] and the rest of the party.

. . . And what with winds that were gales, storms like cyclones, fish-hooks embedded in human thumbs, sailing canoes dumping, dinghies capsizing, snakes joining the family and canines battling under the house with porcupines —what a life they have!

Over the porcupine God knows who screamed loudest, me or Weekes! At midnight it was. Yes, and *under* the house, over boulders, through bushes, tripped by tree roots, stumbling, cursing, yelling and occasionally with a groan, "Oh, where *are* the *boys!*" In bed, of course, in their own shack!

I could always get abreast of the porcupine. The beast moves slowly with its waving armoury. It circled in a sinister fashion, those murderous quills undulating. When at last I caught Weekes up in my arms I was fairly sobbing with exhaustion and fright! I thought my darling would be a mass of the vile barbs. And actually, John, I didn't like

67

the idea that at any moment in the dark I was going to grasp with naked hands that slowly-circling beast! Weekes and I yelled in concert at the poignant discovery that we were *both* too yellow to close with one of the most innocent of the forest creatures! Nothing innocent about the quills, of course. But temperamentally it's a harmless citizen.

> Dahwamah
> Gordon Bay PO, Ontario
>
> Oh John darling—here I am back again, and Dahwamah seems like the Ritz after the camp up there. The Georgian Bay is like a rough sketch of Muskoka. We don't get their furious and long-enduring winds. Our lakes are deeper and more tranquil and haunted by their own ghosts. The water up there is a gay fighting blue, or a river-green. Everywhere it is shallow, and everywhere the sun-bared rocks thrust up—spines and shoulders of rock. The bush is tough and young, and of a very tender green. The pines look stunted after our giants, and the whole country, lying flat in the hot sun and wind, has a wind-bowed look, and everything is rougher and lacks entirely "this is the forest primeval, the murmuring pines and the hemlock...."
>
> Sitting on the dirty little launch that took me as far as the lighthouse I looked at the country ... the wild untamed look of it all, and thought—this is where *we* come in. This is ours. John would adore this. It is the country of anyone who adopts it, and will take its tantrums and like them.
>
> Can you bear it? Oh *John*, it is only because I'd like to *give* it all to you.

But while she was delighting in her country and, as I hoped, building up reserves of health against the possible onslaught which that "pleuritic constriction" never for long allowed me to forget, I was living through the last grim and profoundly saddening stages of the break with Jimmy

Sleator. He was at home with his mother and sister—as I was with mine—in their house at no great distance from ours. His mood was morose, resentful, malicious. For my work, which I was strenuously trying to cope with, I had taken our tiny dining-room and turned it into my writing-room.

The postman came in the forenoon. At about the time when I expected him with whatever he had for me from Primmy, I would sometimes look up and be stricken to see Jimmy's face peering in at me through the window, hostile, tight-lipped, eyes glaring, full of pain—a grotesque and horrible caricature of his natural and normally diffident but pleasantly alert and handsome looks and manner. He was spying—to catch me by surprise as I wrote to Primmy or read what she had written to me. With weary reluctance I would rise and bring him in. To my mother and sister he would be, as he had always been, genial, polite, considerate, allowing them no hint of anything amiss; but in my room and alone with me he was instantly the other Jimmy. He would demand to know if the postman had come, whether he had brought anything from that, that . . . and he would spit out Primmy's name in a spray of epithets of the foulest offensiveness. If the postman had still to come, poor Jimmy would sit on and on, silent, staring, uninvited, determined to await his coming; then, if there should be a letter for me from Primmy, he would insolently demand to know its contents. I could not and never did make any concession whatever to this fearful paranoid offence which sharply incensed me but at the same time made me heart-sick. The natural impulse to rise and order him out of the house was restrained by the knowledge that he was indeed deeply wounded by what he believed to be a base betrayal of a long, mutually advantageous and affectionate companionship—betrayal brought about by my having met and fallen in love with Primmy. But in this he was mistaken. For in fact I had decided before I knew of Primmy's existence that our association had run its course and must end. Its character—that of two independent individuals—had for some time been in process of becoming that of one dominating and increasingly possessive individual, and one individual increasingly but resentfully trying to adjust and accommodate. It had become a relationship which—at peril for me of being virtually owned—had to be steered to an end, the least damaging and painful that I could think of.

I had already told Primmy something of all this, and she had been frightened by it; but she had exacted a promise that I would keep her informed. I felt I had to do so, and did, diverging into it in the middle of a letter I wrote to her on her birthday, September second.

> 68 Campbell Park Avenue
> Belfast
> 2 September, 1935.

My dear—I drank to you today. Had you a celebration? A jolly time? I hope so. For myself birthdays count the same as other days. I don't, in fact, much want to remember that I'm approaching the patriarchal age. Yet really that's nonsense. I was reading yesterday a pamphlet of the Society for Individual Psychology, containing the presidential address by our old friend of *The New Adelphi*, James Young (Dr. James Carruthers Young.) Title: "Neurosis and the Awareness of Declining Years."

Funnily enough, *this* evening was broadcast from London a Canadian program by the "Rocky Mountaineers"—hillbillies in a show supposed to represent a sing-song in a lumber camp bunk-house. It was pretty tough sentimental tosh, in fact boring and bad. One of the songs was "Pretty Redwing."

No more moon shines tonight on pretty Redwing,
The breezes sighing, the night-winds crying....

Fearful yammer.

I want to write you something cheerful, especially now when you'll be, I suppose, getting through the nostalgic gloom of changing back from "Paradise" to Toronto. For me it looks as if I'm properly let in—to sit down here and remain here and do nothing for a long, long time but work, work, work. . . . You see, when one has dodged the necessity of really facing the problem—dodged along, improvising ways of being where one *wants* to be, and doing what one *wants* to do . . . and when at last something occurs which makes him face round quick and sharp to behold the blank *fact* and *need*—fact of no security, need of at least *some* margin of security—and when one isn't the kind of facile go-getter who goes and *gets* all-in-the-morning-early— well then, my dear, the jolly romp's about over. There's the writing-table and there's the chair; and chained Prometheus was in no tighter fix on that rock of his. . . .

Do you think you could tolerate—survive—with me long months, and if months then years of this dreariness? Ah, how far away now is Mayfield! Ever again? Maybe. Miracles *do* happen? They're the reward of the credulous. Oh be credulous then if you can, Primmy. For me, every day is another in the making of a skeptic. Look, darling, do you remember how you used to bully me with your "Come on, I *want* to hear it! Spill it right out!" Well, now I *want* to tell you, but I *do not* want to depress and worry you. Only, per- haps you *ought* to hear what's going on. Because that "cold wind of anxiety" is most dangerous when you pretend it just isn't there.

I won't sink you in this muddy tide again. It's the old tale. How I saw it distress you, time after time! In Regent's Park. In the ABC. In the Dutch Oven. In Shearn's restau- rant. Well, of all days on your birthday, Jimmy came here and his first words were direct, point-blank pistol shots to the heart of the matter about you. We talked about it and talked about it. He went away. Came back again and talked and we went out and walked around and talked. He hasn't adjusted himself to the situation at all, I'm afraid. (Oh Primmy, it's as well there are these months to let adjustment of some sort have a chance.) Jimmy just refuses to accept any change. I will do anything in the world not to hurt him; but the trouble of course is that not to hurt by dodging what has happened would be to do a deeper injury in the end. For the moment nothing is settled about going back to London. Jimmy says he will leave here next week— to go *where?* He doesn't know. It's an unhappy business. Next week something will have transpired. I'll write you fully. Or are you heart-sick and tired of this whole thing? Oh, more than anything else in the world I long to see you fulfilled and happy in your life. You, and Jimmy.

Look, Babs darling, don't get frightened . . . Be *yourself* to me in spite of this. But you can see—I had to tell you. So long, darling   —John.

Yet what was going on was no news to her.

50 Forest Hill Road
Toronto 5
Friday, 13 September.

John dearest, I am sorry—terribly sorry about the whole thing. I'm sending you a cable tonight, whether to comfort you or me I don't know. . . . Oh darling we *are* hacking our way through a jungle, a wilderness, an *uproar.* Mine is that, though a lot better than yours. *And* we'll get there. Don't you see that nothing can stop us except this getting "lost?" That is what's worrying us both.

When I get back—or you greet these shores—we can *talk.* Isn't it funny that the only thing I take any interest in is the thought of you? Which, considering the battle and the din is rather ironic.

I am writing this in the garden, lying down. Lazy? Well, I'm all in. Nice way to tackle the novel isn't it?

Why didn't I talk to you when I had you, I wonder; and why didn't you occasionally listen instead of just looking at me? I left peace on the island with the bit of white jade; but I carry your letters about in my arms, if that means anything! And if you have heard one half of what I have been saying to you, by day and by night...! I am glad you still love me in all this uproar   —Babs.

As I have mentioned, "Babs" was her familiar name in her family, in Toronto. In London it remained Primmy. She looked back to recall the closing of Dahwamah for the season, and the return to Toronto.

> From now on: 50 Forest Hill Road
> Toronto 5

... Wednesday night my weather broke. We had a fire roaring up the chimney. (The fireplace is one of the "show" pieces. Takes up practically one wall—huge rocks left rough as they came, and a great plank of a mantelpiece supported on pine logs. When you fill the cave—the fireplace—with great logs of red cedar—and turn from the fire to see the cold blue of the water, and the frosty glitter of all the stars...!) When the company lit its candles and started to bed I huddled into an overcoat and went down the path to the big wharf—where I tramped up and down, looking at the sky "thick inlaid," and at the reflections in the moving water. What a *night*! Where were you? I was thinking of us.

Getting into the lake before breakfast *these* mornings is a spartan affair. Thank heaven the middle of the day is hot, if you get out of the wind and find some spot where the August sun has haunted a few hours before you get there....

73

We have sailed and sailed, the North wind being friendly in that regard. Spanking blue seas we've had, and a light crew, so the little old dinghy has buried her deck at times in a smother of racing white. *Grand*, John! I *adore* it.

They began talking of the end last week. I looked out into my woods, and was quite shocked at the physical pang that *wrung* my heart. But it is true. And perhaps it's as well one can live just so long picking flowers on the edge of a precipice. Which crypticism I would unravel for you but that it would weary us both.

I am writing to you up in my own room, with the bats squeaking under the eaves. Indeed I think they are right here, *with* me. It's a nice room; one wall all windows, and those windows framing trees and trees—a break in the trees —water. There is a clutter of my belongings, clothes, colours, toys, books, photos, cosmetics—and a few relics that weather all years.

It's taken me practically the summer to read Conrad's *Chance*. What a *book*! If I saw Marlow's photograph on a woman's dressing-table, I would know it at once. And Captain Anthony, too—although I would only expect to find it on Flora's—or perhaps young Rowell's tallboy. What always strikes me dumb with admiration and astonishment is his women—and the easy way he *sees*, past chance or guidance, *through*. Before I took to the sea I read Bibesco's *There is no Return* with a devotion it hardly deserved perhaps; and as I grinned delightedly at every slick scoring, I thought of you—and of how you would let me have it, much as one says to a child, "All right—*eat* sugar pops!" thinking she'll be sick. Still, perhaps—Bibesco, Aldous Huxley, Stella Benson, Conrad, Rainer Maria Rilke—the Notebook —what a course to steer! But it may console you to know that it was with Conrad and Rilke that I really ran upstream for repairs, and stayed, and stayed. The last chapter of *Chance* is headed "A moonless night, thick with stars above, very dark on the water." These nights have been like that. Are you all right, darling? Where are you, then?

—Primmy.

She did not know if I were still in Belfast, or had gone to London. As she was writing that letter to me I was simultaneously writing to her. I had been to the beautiful country along the broad, winding, tidal reaches of the river Foyle between Derry and Strabane. I had last been there for the burial of my Uncle Sam (Samuel Clements) at The Grange, the old burial place of my mother's family. (An illegal burial, The Grange being full and no further burials permitted.) I had told Primmy about it in a letter. As the minister was somberly involving us once more in the ineffable mystery of those ritual words in the committal service, "This corruptible must put on incorruption," I felt a furtive tugging at my coat:

"Take that in your hand sir," the old gravedigger says to me, under his breath, handing me a yellow bone. "D'you know whose that is?"

"Whose?" I asked.

"That's the thigh bone of your Aunt Mary Jane. I mind the day I sunk her here, five-and-twenty year ago."

I looked at it and threw it back into the brown loam piled at the open graveside—and I remembered how that old lady had cuffed me, and been good to me, as a small boy.

68 Campbell Park Avenue
Belfast
Friday 13/9/35
Babs dear, I'm so fed-up, with things that I should simply not write to you at all, rather than write what can hardly fail to be a dismal letter. I've just returned from a very dismal couple of days in the country—visiting old and ailing relatives and doing business for them with country solicitors.

It's outrageous, really, how they have all honoured *me* with the job of hearing their woes and attending to their affairs. Poor old creatures—when they die off I inherit only responsibilities, adding to the already-shouldered burdens. Not anything colossal. But when even a straw is pretty nearly the last straw! Well, darling, should I just not write to you now but wait till I feel happier? Ah, Primmy, when one has struggled with miseries for a couple of days—when one has visited bits of lovely countryside one knew as a child and that should have been still the property of one's family had it not been mishandled and lost—it's enough to excuse the feebleness of sitting down and writing it all to you— my unfortunate darling.

And the critical days have really come, Primmy. I don't know if Jimmy has returned to London. He *was* to go. Opening up the studio by himself will be hard on him. Yet I cannot see what else is to be done. There *is* nothing else to be done. I hope he will find some sort of adjustment possible. But he left me very unhappy in his mind. Primmy, do you think you can stand what may have to be gone through, if unhappiness should lead to active, violent hostility? Maybe I'm unduly pessimistic about what may emerge for us. I do hope I am. But it's as well to know we may have to face rough weather. God, shall we *ever* get this crooked made straight? How I *wish* you . . .

Later:

Precisely as I was about to finish that sentence—"How I wish you were near me," a knock—Jimmy's knock at my door. (I was mistaken in thinking he had gone on to London.) But it can't be a great delay.

This morning I've been surveying the landscape—the sixteen weeks of it stretching ahead till January sixth. (She had planned to return to me in London in January.) It might pay me best to sit here and work and try to get a trifle of cash collected. But I'm for pulling through, and out of,

76

this mess somehow. Keep your courage and your gay and gentle spirit unrattled by anything that those divils of time and tides can hurl against us. By heaven you'll jolly well need to, Babs! *That's* the price of not having stuck to your guns last St. Patrick's day . . . when you startled me with your murmured "Guess I'm not going through with this!"

Enough of this unleavened lump of lugubriousness! "Gathering flowers on the edge of a precipice" did you say? So long, my dear   —John.

But that "cold wind of anxiety" continued to chill my mind; and I had little doubt that Primmy's mind, too, was chilled by it. She was now, for the first time, to admit that throughout the summer months at Dahwamah and the Georgian Bay, while assuring me that she was well and loving the life of sailing and swimming and of enchanted, solitary wanderings around the wooded island shores in her canoe by sun and moon she was in fact terrified that my fears for her, because of that "pleuritic constriction and spat-up blood," might indeed be well founded. She had longed for me to have the peace of mind of believing that she was safely out of that "whirlpool" as she called it, and had longed for me to see her as indeed growing serenely brown and bonny, abrim with health and high spirits. And at least she could withold any admission of her own secret fears until they should be confirmed or confidently dismissed by medical examination and opinion at the highest level—to which she had access through her father's exalted position in his profession.

My own "uproar" with Jimmy did, I felt sure, seriously contribute to the menace of the whirlpool. So did two other nagging anxieties: our lack of means, and the threat of renewed war which at that time was darkening the world.

She had gone to live for a time at the house of her sister Agnes (also known as Jimmy) and Agnes' husband Norman

77

Macdonnell—9 Montclair Avenue, Toronto—a house destined to have an important part in our subsequent life together.

9 Montclair Avenue

Toronto

1/10/35

Darling I know my letters have been a bit hysterical—I can just bring myself to use the word—but I blame it, not on me, nor even on our own particular "jam." I blame it on this war scare. Let me get one thing straight. If you want me, cable for me. If you want to come to me, cable the port of landing and I will meet your boat. We said January. January suits me all right . . . I will stand up to what racket ensues . . . Father will probably balk at my sailing. He might use my late "illness" as a reason for saying don't try wintering in England.

Enough of this illness, anyway. Boiled down, it is this: I did have a slight dilitation of the heart in Muskoka. Did not rest—so, the usual collapse ensued. I was frightened and depressed, thinking it might mean I had stirred up the lung, and three months' rest at someone else's expense would follow. I was in a fairly unapproachable state of mind! You know how stupefying fear is. Dr. Parfitt says he wishes he had a pair of lungs like mine—or words to that effect. They will soon discover I never *had* TB. He can't think why I went "phut," but *I* can. So he has only to sign me up a clean bill, and we'll call it a day. I am bored with it now anyway—and when I am bored I am *really* finished.

I couldn't write yesterday. I could only make sure I *didn't*. I was so cranky. And I *am* lonely. This war—will it stop me getting back to you? I had been forlornly wondering if I was cracked to send that cable. [Assuring me she was well—and cheering for the success of my play *The Family Portrait*.] I simply *had* to do it because the whirl-

78

pool was still boiling all round me—I thought I was going to repeat 1921–1930 [two former serious bouts of TB]. But I waited till I knew my panic was unfounded [on the assurance of Dr. Parfitt, an eminent TB specialist]. I've been feeling such a sweep about letting you know I ever *was* ill. I think I told you primarily to justify myself for being such a fool as to *get* ill, and partly because I couldn't bear you to think that at such a moment in our concerns I was just having a good time. I was *not*.

I hope *you* are well, darling. Please do that bit too. I am so sorry about Jimmy—that's all I can say. Can't you see that he can't frighten me either by writing to me or coming at me with a gun? He can only get at me through you, and he must know that. I know you're unhappy over the break, and I don't see much light through the trees. But I am the daughter of a most unconcerned surgeon. You must show him the patients in the coffin *with* the lilies before he will believe that there is not every chance that they will be as good as ever. So—on no drink—nothing—I work it out sometimes—this quite *im*possible sum, and it comes out quite all right all round. Tell me we'll be together quite soon, will you? I'd send you a cable every morning if I had the cash.   Love from—Babs.

In another letter at about this time she remarked, "My letters may be gloomy from now on—they just reflect where the sun is, and how damp and how cold is the earth." But she did try to dissipate the gloom by talking about the livelier of the authors whose books she was reading. She would diligently quote bits—such as Dorothy Parker's seven-word caustic dismissal of a play she had endured in her work as drama critic, " 'The House Beautiful' is the Play Lousy"; or this, of Dorothy Parker's friend Alexander Woolcott, "All the things I really want to do are either immoral, illegal or fattening." She had a seemingly inex-

79

haustible treasury of such witticisms, and of amusing stories about the wits who uttered them. They were the "light relief" which she had set herself to help make bearable our winter passage. I had been aware too, that in her letters to me from Dahwamah during the summer, along with her own continual assertions that she was well, she included remarks in corroboration—remarks that by implication would convince me that she was indeed successfully riding out the inner storm.

"I am more at peace here than I have been anywhere on this continent since Dot [Dorothy Joy, her adored elder sister] died."

"Elizabeth [her step-mother, Mrs. Primrose] said, 'I have never seen Babs like this. I suppose it is because she is really happy for the first time.' "

"One night we were out in the canoe. . . . Grahame [Dot's widowed husband] said 'You haven't looked like this since long before Dot died. Whoever he is, Babs, marry him and bring him out here.' I couldn't help smiling—so simple as that, eh John?"

Then, a reminder of her oblique sense of humour: her brother-in-law, Norman Macdonnell, a witty and brilliant young lawyer lately become a Justice of the Supreme Court of Canada, had just suffered major dental horrors because of illness. Babs wrote, "I am just going to amuse myself wallowing in gloom! 'Francesse'—well, that's the way they pronounce it—*ruined* my hair, and I cried with rage. I didn't see anything funny in crying about it either. I said to Norman, 'You may think because you have lost for ever all your lower teeth that *you* have a grievance. I tell you—*I* have had my *hair* badly cut!' I suddenly saw how Samson felt when he was tricked and awoke in the camp of his enemies without his mane. I have always been so *glad* he brought down the temple."

On one of our midnight prowls in London before she

sailed, Primmy had remarked that, uncharacteristically, I seemed suddenly interested in clothes. I did indeed admire the infallible rightness-for-her of her clothes, both casual and formal. She knew it, and because of it and of her exquisite femininity which she knew I adored, she spoke of it. An instance: favourite among her relations were the elderly daughters of a former Lieutenant-Governor and Premier of Ontario, Sir Oliver Mowat. Of them she wrote to me, "I have to go and have dinner with Aunt Laura, who is over 80, and blind, and a darling. A cousin of mine, about six or eight years older, Edie Mowat is there—and Aunt Laura's younger sister. I am dressed up to kill. They love it—and oh, *so* do I. Only, darling—it seems a little wasted on anyone but you."

She sent me a little portfolio, in which, to show me something of the glory of Canadian fall, she had mounted a set of richly coloured maple leaves.

68 Campbell Park Avenue
Belfast
11 October, 1935.

Darling, your packet with map and leaves from Dahwamah arrived this forenoon. Those leaves and the way you arranged them were very much a reminder of a queer inconsequential creature I used to know. She had a little room in Dorset Square. . . . When I looked at them a pulse leaped in my heart, and I turned quietly to catch her standing there, and I said her name. And then—well then I firmly thrust my face inside the mask again, the mask I've been wearing so long now that almost I've forgotten which *is* the mask—a rather grim affair, the portrait of a stoic.

Darling, I'm drivelling. Strange—I lapse into this sort of thing only to you. But maybe that's a trick—dodging the things that might get said if I once began to talk straight sense.

Have you any idea yet about what's going to happen—I mean in the new year? Are you *planning* to come back in January? I must write you my own plans—when I have any that can be called *plans*. Things will begin to take shape soon; and I'm less despondent now than I've lately been. . .

John.

Babs too, seemed less despondent—or hoped by the tone and content of her letters that I would think so. To relieve any fears I might have about the heart-strain that had given cause for anxiety in Muskoka, she wrote that at her father's insistence she had consulted his old friend Dr. John Oille, an eminent heart specialist. And I was amused by what she had to say about one of two housemaids—Mabel Bell and her married sister Susan Shaw—who, after training with people I knew in Ulster had arrived in Canada to join the domestic staff of Babs' family.

9 Montclair Avenue
Toronto
16 October, 1935.

This afternoon I called on a bloke about my heart—the same "Oille"—same little viper—little Quaker that I dislike. But it is kind of him to see a "deadhead"—i.e., a non-paying patient. . . . He admitted that it is four weeks too late to find anything wrong with my *heart*. (I'm a wonderfully good patient, I am. If I'm frightened I do, for the moment, what I'm told—and if I like the man I even try to back up his diagnosis, defend his reputation, and put on weight from his prescription. One of their obstacles—I refer to the medical profession—is that I was—that I *am*—an anti-vivisectionist. But I am not very courageous about it.) He says that my heart is okay, always has been, and always should be! So—how's that? I take it all back about him, too, for he was damn kind.

Monday morning:

When I got in on Saturday night I found your two letter-cards. Thanks, darling. I want the long letter, but believe me the scraps are good. . . . Funny, I've always thought those people who wrote to each other every day were mutts! I could not *imagine* what they found to say!

I have to go out and vote, so I shall break my neck (slightly) to be back here by lunch. But I must, you see, because of Mabel. I *want* peace, so I pander to Mabel. She is the best cook I have ever known . . . I am devoted to her, and she to me. So—I can camp down here when I like. I love her stories—Ulster stories—and provided I don't *argue* with her—about the dogs, the house, the kitchen and her family—or religion, or *politics*—I am all right. Isn't it curious that Jimmy [Primmy's sister] *will* talk while I write. People think you can write with less concentration than they give to *knitting*.

It is a heat wave this morning. The wind which on Saturday, up north at Armour Heights, made my ears and whole head, first sing and then ache piercingly, is this morning straight from the south, drenched in sun, and has brought those enormous blue-bottle flies that live on rotting fruit.

Thank you for *The Adelphi*. (I thought your thing in it was . . . perfect. I read it out to Norman and Jimmy on Sunday morning, which was a strain for me.) I was so glad to see it again I could have eaten it.

I'm glad MacLurg [BBC] wrote you a "rather decent letter" about the Quebec program. Knowing your passion for understatement and your horror of "loud speakers" I take it the man was pleased.

A few days ago, feeling very conspicuous in Norman's ex-artillery breeches, a green sweater, a green suede coat, a blue leather long coat, my own boots, a knotted scarf, a green beret, and a few clothes to change into for dinner, I lumbered into "Coles"—with the paper—a sensational

83

Star. I "took in" the war news and (because of it, and as a trained nurse) I decided to apply to the Victorian Order for substitute work (should it be needed). I did that once—a terrible month—June 1926—obstetrical cases and incurables, some slum work, some less slum and much more depressing—$100 per month.

Elizabeth Maclennan [a life-long and very dear friend from nursery-tea days—a lawyer in Toronto after a brilliant career at Oxford] drove up in her new car and brightened life for me. . . . It is hard for the young Joys—who look upon Elizabeth as nice, *very* nice but unattached and very old—to grasp that she *has* a new car and a thoroughbred colt.

There is a sick feeling in my heart suggesting that your letters to me are going to "fall off," and if they do, if they do! my dear man—I am going into a convent at once.

Aloha, Babs.

68 Campbell Park Avenue
Belfast

You say that if my letters fall off you're going into a convent at once. All right. But depend on this—if you do you'll soon be hearing of a first-rate "romance"—in newspaper lingo. It will set all the doting hearts of Toronto frustrates, male and female, but especially female, palpitating furiously, and will give your friend [Gordon] Sinclair something to gush about at the microphone. Can you guess what it will be? It will be a raid on a convent—and next morning's papers will stream a headline. MYSTERIOUS IRISH ADVENTURER CARRIES OFF BEAUTIFUL TORONTO NUN. And the "story" will tell how he had waited and waited and WAITED—till at last over a higher-than-Capulet's wall he climbed and met her there and bore her off—some say to a secret island in the lakes north of Muskoka Lake. Ah, my prophetic soul . . . dream not too precisely on it! That story in whatever shape—it will come true. Am I a monk already for your sake, Primmy? And you a nun for mine? Much love to you darling —John.

As the summer ended and the customary time to return to London arrived, the long heart-searing process of disentangling—the break with Jimmy—also drew toward its end. The miseries which had envenomed every move of every stage of the way thickened to an intensity hardly to be endured—and endured, I sometimes feared, at some risk even to one's sanity. Morning and afternoon and evening, every meeting with Jimmy was a renewed horror—a reckless hurling of recriminations, threats of vengeance: "I've the fire of a tiger in me . . ." to do this or that, invariably followed by pleas, sometimes abject, pitiful: "Oh John, my head's going!" And appeals, distressing, foredoomed appeals to forgive, forget, return together to first happy days of mutual friendship and trust. But I knew that, even in the wholly inconceivable circumstance of my breaking instead with Primmy, any such return had long ago become wholly impossible.

The climax of this desolation came when, by a most unfortunate chance a letter to me from Helen Waddell about Primmy's novel, *Household Accounts*, was forwarded from the studio to Jimmy's house instead of to mine. I never saw the letter. He said he had torn it up, brandishing his fist as he came to fall upon me, white-faced and quivering in a paroxysm of rage, accusing me of having secretly made use of one of *his* friends to help that, that . . . again the spew of foully offensive epithets about Primmy. (In fact, my acquaintance with Miss Waddell had nothing to do with whatever friendship may have existed between her and Jimmy.) After that came a day on which, all day long Jimmy sat in my room saying not a word. He made no reply when I spoke—just continued to sit there, staring; saddening me, for I knew and could do nothing to ease the pain in that accusing stare. In the brooding, intimidating menace of it I could not get on with my writing. I could do nothing but sit there, too, in dejected silence. Occasionally I left the room, hoping that in my absence he would leave. When he did eventually walk out without a word I was utterly exhausted in mind and body, and could have wept both for myself and for him.

The evening of his departure from Belfast arrived. I went to his house and found him sitting, disconsolate, in his room. He would not speak. I went to the window and stood there, gazing out. In the roadway a taxi slowed and stopped at the door. I helped Jimmy carry his trunk downstairs, went with him uninvited to the quays and in a quayside pub drank with him, stout after stout. Little was said. But on the assumption that I, too, might shortly be crossing back to London he asked me to come to the studio. I promised that I would—knowing that in fact I would remain at home in Belfast through the winter unless summoned to London for some consultation with the BBC or on other business concerning my work, an overnight stay of which he need not be aware. We finished our drinks. I went with him to the side of the boat and watched him walk up the gangway and pass out of sight without a backward glance. I was never to see him again. I turned away, grieving—for as Carson McCullers was to say many years later, "the break in understanding, in sympathy, is indeed a form of death." But I hoped that in this parting I had reached the end of an ordeal the most agonizing I had endured. I was soon to find that in this hope I was mistaken.

68 Campbell Park Avenue
Belfast
1/10/35
Jimmy crossed back to London last night—a very deso-

lating departure. It is October. Three months gone! January *is* it? This is a day so bright and warm after a wild night of storm that I walked along with my eyes half-closed in the sun, and suddenly opening them saw something in the contour of the tree-lined road that was—Weybridge. For a moment I half thought you were beside me walking round from the tennis courts. A moment. No, she's in Toronto . . . and I am here! Here until. . . ? When days like this come again it will be spring. Spring, Primmy! Does it mean we'll be together again? This time for good?

Ah but for God's sake let's talk with circumspection. I'm beginning to see this business in a considerably less hectic way now. I think it will all come straight some time. Anyhow with me it's a case of "come what come may . . ." And for you also, I feel, the hectic bother of it is abating. I hope so anyway, for the sake of sanity and peace.

Are you getting down to your work—your novel? If not —let's just say goodbye and quit—right now.

8 October.

J, writing from the studio, remains deeply aggrieved and embittered, and seems to be just brooding on it. In that state he might do anything. I hope he will not write to you anyway. I hope that by my keeping away from London entirely now he will gradually begin to feel less acutely what has happened. He found a scribbled draft of the cable I sent you to the Empress. I had carelessly left the thing lying about in the hustle of that week when he had left London and I was swotting Quebec stuff after your departure. It gave J a shock, I think. He asked me had I done it on purpose— left the draft. Of course not. But now I think it is well the truth about us has been openly declared by that word in the cable—"darling."

I have never allowed myself to be catechised about our

pact. Nor shall I discuss it except with whom I choose. I am sure it has been best, in the circumstances with J, to avoid the direct avowal and permit the implications to speak for themselves. The draft of the cable has done what must have seemed callous had I deliberately done it. How momentous, how sad and tragic even, all this appears to me while it is an immediate, felt realization of the state of affairs—and how deplorable, mistaken and unreasonable when it is a situation looked at with whatever detachment one can achieve! Yet it is upon the deliberate act of judgment that one must finally rely . . . I have no alternative. It remains only to go one's way with as little as possible of hurt or obstruction to anyone else. Unfortunately for us all, with Jimmy it is direct impulse, act-sequence intellectually uncriticized. As he said himself, he "has no thoughts." He has emotional depth and tenderness, flowering into loveliness of every kind while the circumstances favour— and wilting into bewildered embitterment when circumstances turn counter. That's J's make-up. A very precious thing I would do anything not to harm.

See, darling, what thoughts batter my heart these days and nights. And I must speak of them to someone. To you.

One other person I have at last confided in about this— my younger brother James, who lives with his wife here in Belfast. Yesterday I told him, for the first time, about you. We talked. Oh darling what a relief it was to me! We talked quite freely and went over the whole circumstances —or as much as my pact with you permits. I showed him snaps, and the Reprographs. At first I was diffident, and kept my pride in you where it has been from the first—in my heart. James thinks we'll get through. He's sure we must do our best to get through. Primmy—I was glad, so glad, of his friendliness—his welcome of you.

That's my brother James and my sister Annie, of St. Leonard's, rallied to our flag. And with that to cheer us—

shall I just stop now? So long, then, my darling. So long
—John.

With this letter I enclosed an early snapshot of James taken behind the stables of my father's house, Crieve. He is holding a horse—one of two owned by my father at that time, his only extravagance, his customary indulgence of the kind being merely possession of a high-stepping spirited pony. This horse had all but killed me or maimed me for life, having in a sudden alarm, wildly bucked and thrown me in my effort to prevent him from rending himself on a high fence of rusted barbed wire. I told Primmy of the horrible picture that was still vividly in my mind: of myself on my back, feet in the air, the belly of the rearing horse poised above me and his front hooves about to strike my face. I barely managed to escape—with only a long scoop of flesh torn from along my shin bone by the descending hoof. The scar is with me for life. He was a handsome and mettlesome animal. When he first arrived with us my father had said to me, "Throw your leg across him and see what he's like." I have never since had the smallest wish to throw my leg across a horse—although my father's family all loved— and his brothers bred—horses. I told Primmy of this since she herself loved horses and rode them with panache, a fearless and skilful show-jumper.

9 Montclair Avenue
Toronto
Date uncertain, but early October.

Thank the powers for your younger brother anyway. Give him my love. I love the old snap of him and that horse. I'm sorry the brute nearly killed you—and he looks such an angel in the picture, too! Darling I'm sorry about Jimmy. I won't talk about it tonight. I can't. I feel simply wrung out—and I am so terribly sorry for him. And I know I am not worth your losing him   —Love, Primmy.

Helen Waddell was in Belfast during the weekend. She told me that she had really been very much amused by your story and thought it very well done indeed—thought the women's letters—oddly enough—not so well done as the men's. And she thought a little more of the *story* was needed for sales purposes. But she was quite sincerely patting you on the back—hoping you'd not be discouraged but would go on. I told her you were going on. She said she would send you a letter, c/o me, to tell you how much pleasure you'd given her, and that you are one of her kind. She remembered the names of the people [in *Household Accounts*]. See what that implies, Primmy.

There hasn't been time for her to get back to London and send the letter. I'm sure she'll send it and you'll get it at once. She had written before, she told me, sending it to you, c/o me, at the studio. I never saw that letter. (Jimmy had destroyed it.) She said she'd write it afresh! H. W. is a woman facing more trouble than an artist such as she is should ever have to face—or so I surmise. I think her visit here had to do with members of her family who count on her. Ah but sure that's the way with most of us! She's a woman of mettle.

Look my darling—don't, I beg of you, don't be getting under the weather. Don't let yourself go—we *are* going to be together again, and quite soon. . . . My heavens above, sweetheart, how do you think we should get through what we'll have to get through time and again after we *have* come together, if we haven't the resolution and courage to stick this bad bit out? It is bad. But we shall have worse. A lot worse. I wish to God I was near you so that I could go round and hold you out of it all awhile. I don't want to have to tackle last-resort, panic-bred problems—but if I felt you were slipping dangerously I'd risk every disaster and go out to you—out on the first boat.

I may go out sometime. I don't know. The prospects in Canada seem almost nil. Over here, I do know how to pull down the minimum—though it might fail anytime. But I know nothing whatsoever about the conditions over there. "150,000 unemployed young men," I see by one report.

Here's how it is: I am slogging hard at stuff designed to bring me in some cash—next February! (If that succeeds we'll have enough for a Middle House visit!) The moment it's finished I have to blaze into something to meet the racket of December and January. It's a terrible and unremitting fight. But I must admit I sometimes manage to dramatize it to myself to the extent of throwing back my head and laughing through clenched teeth in a kind of ecstatic-hysterical don't-care-a-damn enjoyment of it. But, my God, what a *bloody* fight! "My head is b—— but unbowed"— as the curate wailed in the parish magazine after the wigging over the Harvest Festival decorations with the rector's wife. . . .

About the whole problem of *how* and when we're to put an end to this heart-breaking separation, I'll get a chance to clear my head for a good think—and then, a sensible letter. Will you hold steady and hard till then, my dear? Will you? Come, Primmy, you know this is the sort of help I need from you now. And I know—don't I know!—what it costs. Damn it, it costs me just as much. Only I'm tougher fibred than you, my darling. But—so long, darling—John.

That Primmy should know that at least Helen Waddell had liked *Household Accounts*, and know it before this letter could reach her, I cabled the gist of it. But I understood the implication of Miss Waddell's hope—that Primmy should "not be discouraged"—to be, that Constable took the same view as Methuen—*Household Accounts*—yes, but only after publishing a first novel of a less élite, more popular kind.

9 Montclair Avenue
Toronto
29 October, 1935.

John dear, I'm so pleased about Helen Waddell. It's probably only because she's keen on you—but still—*wow!* Isn't it nice? I haven't told anybody about it, because they don't know what it means to get patted on the back by her. Probably all for you, as I keep on telling myself.... Thank 'ee, darling.

I wish you weren't working—driving quite so hard. There isn't any other way, I know. But somehow it's wrong, it's cracked—that you *should* be. And one of the main furies is that it's not in Belfast but in *London* you should be now, cashing in on the footing you have with the BBC. And yet I dread London for you, as I could never dread it for myself ... John darling, I'd help about Jimmy if I could—and while we're separated I'll do what I can. I know it wouldn't really help if I was there now, where you could come and see me. And I couldn't stand seeing you torn to bits before my eyes—not again!

Darling I want this Christmas at home. I have planned and schemed for it. I never now count on more than one Christmas ahead; I who used to count nothing "settled" until every day of seven years ahead was allotted!

Don't lambaste me too hard about my new novel. I want to burn a few boats first. Don't you see—I want to get clear and I know as well as you do that the novel is my only hope —our only hope. Actually I've done what I knew I *should* do. I've applied for work—in four different directions, because I can't face that melancholy burning of the boats. But if I get through *that*, then I can start my novel; and if I *know* I have a job and a pay-cheque waiting—I can get through *that* by the good old Policeman Time method.

Darling, ever since you first heard about the whirlpool—or rather heard what it *was*—and if you ever really gathered what it was—you are a miracle-man . . . an angel about writing. But I don't *want* you to carry any *more* than you're carrying, so don't load yourself down with me, too. I'm really all right now. The little Quaker [Dr. Oille] gave me *iron* in no uncertain form. It always amuses me the way the medical profession "have" you. You say, "No I won't rest!" "No, I don't need any care!" So they, with the most gentle of grins, give you something strong enough to knock you down! But—*vive* iron and Oille anyway! It's given me a little more *control* and I needed that . . . I have been as edgy as a bear, and as unreasonable as anyone crossed in love!

Thank you darling for all the absurd, ridiculous and grand things you've been saying, lately. I try not to believe them—and when I remember it's *you* saying them, I half don't. But they're exhilarating anyway
—Love from—Primmy.

The absurd, ridiculous, but grand things Babs said to me I, too, found exhilarating. I told her:

"I read your letters over and over again, and think, 'I knew I was right, I knew!' When you say such things as, 'The thought of you means peace for me,' I feel exhalted and incredulous, and rather frightened and ashamed. Oh darling are you wholly irresponsible and blind and quite a fool? I think you must be. Maybe that is why, in spite of judgment and every hostile circumstance, I still believe I may find you wanting me when the "uproar" of all the tides and times has dwindled. Only—I've no right to let you. No right—and yet I should be desolated if you took me at my own valuation and made yourself stop wanting me. . . .

"I had thought at first that your references to a 'whirlpool' meant some dispute with your people . . . about me, perhaps, or your plans for the winter. I thought your "uproar" was something of the same kind as my own. Maybe it's as well I was wrong. Dilated heart can be ministered to. Distracted mind isn't so easy. I called mine a thicket. You called yours a jungle. *You* are through, for the moment. I, being left here in Belfast while Jimmy has gone back to London, am not by any means through. But there are at least intervals of comparative lucidity and peace. I will do all I know to get the lucidity and peace extended until some kind of sanity returns to existence for all of us. Otherwise—well I don't want to anticipate the "otherwise." You've had an unfair lot of it to put up with already anyhow. As though you were in any way to blame, for anything. Nobody's to blame. This is simply the kind of revenge life sometimes takes on people who have insisted on playing the game by their own rules."

I knew that Babs had read widely, in verse, fiction, literary essays; so her forthright rejection of a suggestion that she read Middleton Murry's *Socialism 1935*, surprised me.

50 Forest Hill Road
Toronto
5 November, 1935.

... You know darling, I am *far* more interested in *Grey Owl* than I could ever be in Middleton Murry, Havelock Ellis, T. S. E. and Bertrand Russell. ... Do you remember once telling me as we were walking toward some bus in Holborn that you had waded through an enormous amount of reading, because, although you didn't care about it, specially, Murry was interested, and you thought enough of him to do it *on that account?* I sighed at the time. Murry was awfully decent to me. But ... And *Grey Owl's* a good book—the photographs are, anyway! I am reading—not *Socialism 1935*, but nursery rhymes. I always do. I wrote

you—pages of explanation of this (very natural) prefer-
ence. Thanks be I didn't send it! . . . Our celebrated Vien-
nese Dr. Adler—who *discovered*, so they tell me, the
Inferiority Complex—would urge me to "come clean." I
will, Juggens, in *time*. . . .

Tell me, is *Top Hat* in Belfast—the Astaire–Ginger
Rogers film? Because you go, darling. Go because it'll make
you laugh. . . . If I was generous I would add take someone
else in my place, but I'm not . . . though I don't think we
can get out of it now! Is that any comfort to you? You see,
I am so sublimely and inescapably vain that it hardly occurs
to me with any force—that you are trying to be "the one
that got away!"

I have had peace, John darling, peace . . . I am here all
alone with A. Primrose [her father]. Sorry you don't know
him, for you and he would get along fine. I think he is
secretly grateful to you for even *thinking* of taking me
away. But on the other hand I am his youngest . . . he has
never seen me belong to anyone, and been convinced.

. . . Friday night we had The Earthquake! Have you
heard of it? It was a good joke, but like so many good ones
not in the best of taste. *No* damage . . . no loss of life—but
all the fireworks. The stories about it are quite worth that
horrible three minutes' fear. They are gloriously funny—
and true.

I was in bed, lying on my back and dreaming—a thor-
oughly nasty deception-cum-suspicion-cum eavesdropping
nightmare. In fact when I woke to feel the bed shuddering,
I was relieved. I was so damn glad to say "It's only a
dream." But the shaking got worse and worse, and the windows and doors rattled . . . I thought "This is a bit steep.
Rather have the dream any day." Fool! It's Chips, under
the bed—clever pup to get through two closed doors. . . .
No, it's the furnace . . . it's an earthquake! Then it's goodbye! Oh it *is* goodbye! Oh, *very* comic! I thought of you,

John, and fairly whimpered, "I'll not have the luck to be killed, only half-killed, crippled." I got up and opened the rattling, hammering, thumping door. Mabel (the cook) poor soul, was alone in the big attic, with Chips who *barked* at the earthquake. The door leading from the upstairs hall opened, and Mabel in her high, terrified treble said, panting for breath, "Oh—it's—an—*earthquake!*" And Jimmy [Babs' sister] who had got *her* door opened, said, in a well-really-sometimes-you-do-go-too-far tone, "Oh *Mabel!*" I said, in dismal confirmation, "It's an earthquake, all right!" I walked with trembling knees down into the hall. "Well don't go *down*, dear!" says Jimmy. "I'm going to look at the furnace," I said with dignity. But the gauge for the oil furnace was as low as I felt...!

That letter—about *The Adelphi* and "our" affairs—I'm holding it!

You are a blessed lunatic—and it's ridiculous but I still seem to love you!   —Babs.

50 Forest Hill Road
Toronto 5
14/11/35

Well darling, my hands are so cold I can hardly write—this very hour the Indian Summer took flight. I am sitting up in the Junk Shop [her attic room] tasting peace. I wish you would walk in. Would you mind just walking in?

I shall be alone here with two Finns (house-maids). Ah such cooking! And two cars, and David [Dr. Primrose's "man"—and chauffeur). But I will not be driven—much. I can still walk, and one is more likely to get work *on foot*.

My temper is not what it was. I mean it was once so good! Now, I find after a day cadging for work I am ready to throw boots at my old pals. Lucky to still have boots to throw! I think it is very likely that I shall be serving the Great Public—looking into their unwashed, or over-made-up, or moron-like faces from December first to December twenty-fifth. I toted up my bills and it seems the easiest way out. Surely, *surely* I can bear it for a few weeks! Besides, I might enjoy it? —My love, Babs.

She did take a temporary "Christmas rush" job—selling books, but also other Christmas presents. I feared the effect on her of the physical strain, for in spite of all her assurances my anxiety about her health persisted. I wrote again urging her to cut all else and concentrate on writing the new novel. I also sent a series of letter-cards, which she called scraps, about this-and-that of an encouraging kind; and with them the letter from Helen Waddell about *Household Accounts*. Something in the way I had addressed the letter to her alarmed her—led her suddenly to fear I had left Belfast and gone back to London to be, as she had put it, torn to pieces.

50 Forest Hill Road
Toronto
16 November, 1935.

Oh John darling, your scraps and the H. W. enclosure swung the day. But *what* a day. It shows you the state I was in, that I stared with horror at the writing of my name and "Britannic" on the envelope. I thought—well, this *does* finish it. Something's happened. I'll have to go over. Now! He's ill! He's left a letter in Belfast to be forwarded. No, he hasn't—*he's* written the address. . . .

About five minutes later I sat down—to withstand the shock better!—and found what I had completely forgotten was ever coming, Helen Waddell's letter. I couldn't read it, didn't attempt to anyway till I had eaten up every word of the scrap. That was a cocktail, that was! I spent about twenty minutes trying to read what H. W. had said. . . . Yes, it's a grand letter. What else would it be! . . . I am

97

absurdly pleased to have all these pages in her handwriting. It all reminds me of the reviews of *Peter Abelard.* . . . She must be a saint to go to all that trouble *twice.* Or else she's very keen about you. Try as I will I do *not* think it was my "light relief" that got it. [At this time she regarded her writing as in the nature of light relief.] But thank you John, my dear lunatic, ever and ever so much. If you had read *Pink Furniture* you would see what I mean by lunatic. [I had teased her again about her devotion to nursery rhymes.] Ah, darling, what shall I *do?* They are the only things I can read when I am low in my mind and anxious—these kids' books. But listen, John, I did write *Household Accounts* in seven weeks. . . .

Do *you* remember the day you looked at me—putting it mildly—a bit ferociously and said, "By —, if I had hold of you, you'd *work!*"? Because if you don't remember it, I *do.* It tickled me at the time—but it also scared me a bit. I thought, "He *means* that!"

You say, "The best response to H. W.'s letter is the new book." All right—but remove some of these mountains, will you? Remove the temptation of escaping into the whirlpool—of selling Christmas books and being solaced and doped with a pay-cheque every Thursday; remove Dot's children for they weaken me; remove Forest Hill for I love it: help me burn these boats and clear the Junk Shop for action and promise me that I shall have something more than a headache and a sheaf of charitable remarks when I am done. . . . Don't you *see* that I have never done otherwise than carry it [her writing] as a side-line—which, as Leonard Huxley pointed out, and Murry pointed out, I was so damned lucky to be able to do?

All this—balderdash! It must be because I am alone in the house—and lonely for you, I suppose. But between your letter and H. W.'s I see what you mean. And I will. But listen: I can't write things over. Can't revise. If I don't clear the fence first time I try, I may as well try another jump farther on, because I only muck up the ground going at it again.

The reason why I didn't write on the hospital years ago is because I was too beaten and sore. [I had urged her to write out her three-years' experiences while a nurse-in-training.] I'll tell you the other side of those three years, sometime. The only time in my training that I nearly passed out of the picture, was when I was in the Public Nursery. We were so short-handed that I went into the *Case Room* to collect my own babies—which was against the rules. My two twin boys. Both of them died. For a long time I brooded over this—and cried—and my hand got so shaky I could not put the silver nitrate in the new babies' eyes! Oh, stupid and irrelevant display of emotionalism and self-pity!

I nursed all night—wrote while on night duty; I rode all day in the Horse Show, and slept in the tram. I wasn't a good enough nurse to get away with any side-lines. On finishing at the Vic [Royal Victoria Hospital, Montreal] my "graduating" involved me in one long speech—in verse, if you'll believe it! I put on two plays, and took over the Year Book—and paid for my versatility. [She just missed the coveted Gold Medal.] Did you ever read Barbellion's *Journal of a Disappointed Man*? Do you remember his awful brooding and probing over his dismal heart? I laughed at that full-page article on the heart you sent me. I nearly sent you—just as it stood—my third-year paper on "Cardiac Compensation." But that seemed a punishment in excess of your crime.

You say in your letter, "It's no good asking you questions which are asked to elicit an answer." I daresay. On the other hand I do write you from 9.20 till 11 PM with hardly a breather   —Primmy.

With the approach of Christmas and New Year I began to

doubt that our long-planned and repeatedly promised re-union would indeed be possible: I feared that after all she would not be coming back to me in January. This doubt was strengthened by a suspicion that I had not been hearing the whole truth about her actual or threatened serious illnesses, nor about the trend of her struggle to choose between a painful uprooting from family and familiar friends and places in the pleasant, leisured well-founded life in Canada —and a hazardous, financially ill-founded life of hard work with me in London or in Ireland. Five days before Christmas I had heard from her of the day-long strain of that "temporary job"—the over-heated shop [Mrs. Young's Little Shop Round the Corner in Toronto], the sore feet, the splitting head.... We had exchanged Christmas presents —though I disliked as much as she revelled in the Christmas hysteria—revelled in it at least in so far as it was still an innocent joy for the very young amid the adult public's gross commercial festival of sales in the shops, and day and night passionate gluttony at home. She had sent me also, in a balsam-scented small round box made by Indian women of birch bark decorated with stitching of porcupine quills, a minute bear standing erect, carved in wood though not the size of the nail of my little finger. With it was a note characteristic of her feeling for such things:

I picked up this bear in Lausanne in 1921. He has lost a paw. His brother, who was on all fours, got away long since. I love him; and, as he is so small, thought you would take him in.

I did, and I have him with me now. I wrote to her that because of him I would resign my presidency of the Society for the Suppression of Father Christmas.

68 Campbell Park Avenue
Belfast
Sunday, 29/12/35

Babs, my dearest, here at last I've come to the last mail of the year. How many more mails before they'll be needed no longer? How I wish I were writing to say, Blessings on you, darling, for coming back to me . . . now we'll be together—for keeps. Yes, that's what I'd *like* to be writing to you, now within two days of January. January! You said January. Do you remember? "January be it then. But no longer! No longer! I couldn't bear it!"

Since then I've been peering ahead toward January, making my way toward it through such a deadly jungle—the London jungle—and half-aware all the time that when I did reach it the journey might only start forward all over again. I didn't want to admit that to myself. Nor do I want now to admit it. But I'm not so completely bedithered as not to see how we're fixed. You'll come when you can. The interlude has been long—but it was not too long for the necessities of my affairs—as well as yours. And we must stick out whatever extra bit is still needed.

But what a whoop of joy I'd give, to see you coming to me! . . . I *know* I'm insane about it. It's mad. Impossible. But I don't care. I know how soon the last chance of happiness will fade out finally—and rather than accept *this* way of going on I'd turn anywhere and risk anything. We'll be under the sod anyhow in a few years, if not before, so— what the deuce! Those daffodils are *not* going to bloom late on your grave, my dear. At least they'll bloom under our feet this once—your feet and mine; and the place will be by Catsfield Church in Sussex. Oh, it's all planned. I swore last spring we'd see these daffodils together in the coming spring. Well, let's.

Remember what you wrote to me from Dahwamah? How it seemed so senseless, cruel, our separation—"it defeats philosophy." Do you find philosophy a better match for it now, my dear? I don't. Well, that's how I *feel*. But reason —irrelevant as it seems at this moment—reason suggests as probable that soon the urgency of this felt need will pass, and in its stead the cool, the stoic mood will summon up again the old philosopher in *me* also! And maybe I'd better set about recovering that mood at once? ... I think we must decide to meet before *too* long—or say: It can't be done. ... But this remains—you *have* contrived before to reach this part of the world, and stay a year. Primmy, let's see what we can do with your next year. If *you* can be secure for that, or something of that, length of time, I think we'll do it with each other after all! ... God knows we'll need every shilling we can earn between us. So I *must* work— and that's the curse of it—of this 3000 miles between: I want to be calling out to you and to hell with work. ... So long, dear. I'll sit up and work a couple of hours later. So long.

Monday, 30/12/35. 10.30 PM

And I did. I sat up till much too early this morning. Maybe that's why I've been in such filthy form all day. Troubled sleep. Ominous, undefined, dream-fantasies ... Mabe it was because of talking to you so much about the risks I'm dragging you into!

You said in one letter—but not very firmly—that you could come to me in Ireland. Why do I mention this now? Because this ill-starred day finishes with the realization that I *may* not be able to do anything else but stay in Ireland for some time. ... I tell you this because ... Jimmy is entirely unreconciled, and I'm afraid worse than that: as he repeatedly threatened, "London will not hold the two of us. Certainly not *three* of us. That is quite definite." But my decision has been made and nothing will make me go back upon it. I am your man—for as long as you and I live and you still are fool enough to want me. ...

I might go back to London and fight this out at once. But that needs money. And for money I must work. And I can't do work without peace. And for four months I've had hardly any peace. . . . I shall have to stay here—or at any rate stay out of London—till I can school myself to work and get some cash collected. I don't know how long it will take. But that's the shape of things to come, for weeks certainly, perhaps for months. . . . So when you return, Primmy, I may still be stranded here; but that will *not* prevent my meeting you.

Do you think we'll finish 1936 together? We *may* you know! But—goodnight, darling. Goodnight for now.

Tuesday, 31 December, 1935. 2.40 PM

Well Babs, my pet . . . my impulse was—still is, a bit—to withold these pages, and probably burn them. But maybe you'd better have them, all considered. . . . And you did once say, "I'm coming back to you—or you're coming here. And I think we may be all right. . . ." "I'm coming back to you." Oh Primmy, *can* it be true? What? In spite of everything? I'll go up to some church and light four candles for you, one for each letter of your name, B. A. B. S. And I'll say a novena to St. Brigid for you—St. Brigid, who was good always, and fed the birds, and was most kind to the most unworthy, and made of the dumb animals adoring friends, so that her gentleness was a legend among all living things.

And if it has to be in Ireland—or anywhere leagues from London—if we could be together for that bit—"our bit"—isn't *that* what's important?

And then—"Or you're coming here." Maybe I will. How if we make a bid to trek west some day—to BC, say—after you'd come here and we just fixed up with each other no matter what?

But I mustn't start fantasizing! So long my dear—John.

As the midnight silence of 31 December, 1935 was suddenly shattered by the cacophonous clangour of mill horns, ships' sirens, church bells bringing people all over Belfast out to their front doors to shout New Year greetings, I had paused, in what I was writing, to scribble to Babs. I thought of the minister at the Methodist Watch Night service solemnly saying, "The year nineteen-thirty-five has passed into eternity—the year nineteen-thirty-six is upon us. Let us rise and sing: "Come let us anew, our journey pursue. . . ." 1936—and I was in pursuit of perhaps the most important stage of my life's journey.

Three weeks were to pass before I had from Babs her hurried, slightly distraught reply to that last three-in-one letter.

50 Forest Hill Road
Toronto 5
Monday, 13 January. 7.40 PM

John darling, I've got an hour to write to you. Last collection up here, in these select wilds, is 8.40. The post office —the main—three miles south on Adelaide Street keeps open till 10 PM. But it's a bitter, thankless night—ice underfoot and a cold hurricane blowing. This habit of racing three miles south with your letters tells on the old soul in the end. So I think I'll have to make this 8.40 do. And these are no letters to dash off an answer to in a hurry, either. John darling, I don't seem to know the answer any better than I ever did. Ah, listen, darling, I just don't *know* what to do. Ergo, I cannot *think* what to say. But I am not as completely dense as not to realize—dimly—what you have been having these months. The gods probably do not care about me one way or another. They see, even if I cannot, that I am not worth it, so they are—have been up till now —on my side. *I* get the soft time. You have been having what, as far as I can gather has always been yours—undiluted hell.

I keep out of this Jimmy business for two reasons: 1. It isn't my concern, my affair, my business. 2. I haven't, obviously, grasped what it means. You knew that. There is something missing in my make-up anyway. What is it? I could say a lot on this subject. Some day you'll probably have quite a bit to say yourself!

I read those pages with my heart sinking, I admit. It's impossible for me to care terribly about Jimmy's tragedy, perhaps because I *can't* get there, mentally. But I do see what it means in plain fact. It means that I precipitated a crisis that you might have kept away for life. You might have broken with him without this ghastly war between you—and it has crippled you financially and artistically— if it hasn't maimed you.

Oh John, this business of writing letters is pretty bad. Not that we distinguished ourselves by much clear thought and constructive planning when we were together! I blame myself, bitterly. Oh *lord*—"I blame myself." What a line to go on repeating! I behaved as usual, i.e., I wandered on in a happy dream, and pushed the nasty future—the uncompromising, hard and vindictive factual future—away. Not far away; but far enough so that the dream was only shaded by it.

Don't ever blame yourself about me, darling. You haven't hurt me—if I run into all sorts of weather because of our affair it is *my* fault—"fault"—another good word! What I mean is—I brought it on myself. We've been *happy* together. You can't expect much in this strange world. *I've* had so much—that's what is unfair. Don't you see—that if you blame yourself about me I start in on *myself* about you. And I have had some of that already.

I am appalled. There's no use saying I'm not. Because it is such a heavy line-up against you, and you are alone. You were torn to bits by the mess of Dorset Square *v.* Studio last

time. But you *had* Dorset Square, and it built you up a little.
Time's up, dearest. The last of your letter was *lovely.* I
loved it. Take care of yourself. There is a bit—if it's the
smallest bit in creation—coming to us, and we'll have that,
won't we?

Goodnight, darling. The beastly clock thinks I've missed
this mail. May it be wrong!   —Babs.

In saying, "I don't seem to know the answer any better
than I ever did," and "this business of writing letters is pretty bad," she was reiterating frequently exchanged groans;
as, for example, by me in a letter to her (26 October):
"Isn't it a low-down scurvy trick that's been played on us, or
that we've played on each other—3000 miles, a wilderness
of empty weeks, an eternity of waiting—and the uproarious
jungle, a-bristle with sinister threatenings set close in round
us all the time! *A bas!* . . . It's folly. Arrant folly. Let
people love and be together—while the distemper lasts—
and otherwise be coolly sensible and stay apart. D'you know
I think this letter-writing is a subtly treacherous sort of—
substitution. A turning of one's thoughts and feelings toward—the kiss that isn't forthcoming. The object of it, not
being there to compensate, respond, console, must be *imagined*—a kind of ghostly spiritual masturbation. . . . This
afternoon I feel contempt for every check of sense or prudence. Essential only that we come together and let what
happens damn well happen. *That's* my reaction now. But
even at this impatient reckless moment, a wretched fellow
—probably cracked or a phoney Gospel evangel—passes my
window, trailing a wretched infant and wailing out, 'Oh
Cal-va-ree! Oh Cal-va-ree!' Oh *Christ!* I could crucify
him, that fellow, for his mock-pious slimy wail. And yet—
there's that wretched kid with him, warning that when the
moon was up distemper kindled, and in 'contempt for every
check of sense or prudence'—see above—*he* 'let what hap-

pens damn well happen!'

"Prudence or petulance, it'll come to the same sum in simple arithmetic. The facts—which you and I pretend never to have seen, perhaps because they're so *obviously* there—the so-plain facts are: (a) If you're dependent on the family—they have a right to bid you pipe what tune they please. (b) I can't see them deciding that your coming to me, marrying me, is a suitable tune for you and them to dance to. (c) For a time, at least, you should—for all the reliance you could put on me—have to depend a good deal on the family.

"My brother James says, 'Find out just what you've got between you. Pool it. Look for a tiny cottage outside London. Risk it. Try how it goes. You're both completely unconventional—stick it till summer comes, then make for that Muskoka island you're so daft about . . .' I shut him up with a shout, 'Damn it, I know already what we've got between us—NOTHING. NOTHING AT ALL! Got that?'

" 'That's not hard to get,' says James. And there ends our consultation."

Almost three months had passed since I sent that letter. Neither for the present or the future had there been any mitigation in the uncertainties of our predicament. I was still unsure of the answer to that question I had posed, "Do you think you could tolerate—survive—with me long months of this dreariness?" Given that she indeed had the will to tolerate, had she the physical strength to survive it? In anxiously pondering this question I could not ignore a deep suspicion that her repeated assurances that she had the will and the strength might be, in part at least, a stratagem to hold the issue in suspense awhile. Would, *could*, she come to me? If not, must I, *could* I, somehow contrive to go out to her? I had braced myself for six months of separation—July to January—but had barely been able to endure it. Now it was mid-January. Her return was being postponed

—a postponement in what I feared might be but the first in a series of postponements leading to an end which I simply dared not contemplate, for my impatient need to have her back with me was becoming unbearable. I had once written to her, "I may go out sometime. I don't know. The prospects in Canada seem almost nil." This implied the possibility that I might pull up roots in London and Belfast and attempt to put them down in Canada. But the more I knew of it the more the struggle to earn a living as a writer in Canada dismayed me. It dismayed me not only because of those "150,000 unemployed young men" out there but also, and more discouragingly, because of what I found in the huge parcel of Canadian newspapers and magazines which, at my request, Babs had sent me. She had also sent cuttings about radio programs. Except for *Saturday Night, Canadian Forum* and the university quarterlies their generally half-literate and blatantly sensation-mongering contents seemed to promise no place for the kind of contribution I could offer. Short of seeking to attach myself as a staff-writer to one of the daily newspapers I saw no likelihood of being able to make a living—and for journalism of that kind I had neither the wish nor the aptitude.

Babs was herself having some success in book-reviewing, usually for *Saturday Night*. (B. K. Sandwell, from the county of Suffolk—whom I was later to know as The Beak, because of his formidable nose—an able editor discernibly in the tradition of Massingham and Orage, perceiving what Babs could do, entrusted her with the reviewing of unusual books such as Arthur Calder Marshall's novel *Dead Centre*. She sent me a copy of the draft of her review and told me what had happened to it on the way into print. It is before me now as I write. Having read her report one knew what to expect from the book. One also sensed the pleasure it had given her. Yet for her work that pleasure was her chief reward.) She was also having success—in so far as it can be considered success—in selling short stories to such papers as the Toronto *Star Weekly*. The editors of that journal would come upon some photograph of a striking nature that could be used as a front-page coloured feature, providing they could find a story to which it would be the illustration. Babs would be called in. Could she think of such a story, write it, and have it back to the editors within, say, 24 hours? If the photograph engaged her she had an extraordinary facility in imagining and writing at speed the needed story. And she found exhilaration in doing so, although she knew she was misapplying and probably damaging her talent, and though the fee of so many cents a word would do little more than pay for to and fro fares on the streetcar.

In disregard of fears for her physical condition which in retrospect surprises me, I wrote proposing a venture which I knew to be physically taxing, but which would test Babs' ability in descriptive reporting and be better paid than such literary journalism as book-reviewing. Along with a copy of the current *Radio Times* which carried a photograph of me with a piece about one of my plays, I sent—as examples of such descriptive reporting—cuttings of a series of articles I had done dealing with nightly activities essential to the life of any large city: those of street-cleaning, gas works, electric generating stations, hospital, harbour. . . . The series title: *While Belfast Sleeps*.

68 Campbell Park Avenue
Belfast
3 January, 1936.

Darling:

I send you various cuttings. (1) A *Radio Times* scream —a photograph of myself, or alleged to be of me. I thought you'd like to know how they do traduce your long-suffering lunatic. (2) A set of old Belfast *Telegraph* cuttings. I send these for a definite purpose—to put *you* on to a lot of dollars which you ought to be able to pick up by transposing those articles into terms of Toronto: "*While Toronto Sleeps. A Civic Service Series, by O. C. Primrose.*" I did them to make some cash—in 1931, I think. They turned out very popular. So popular that they were hawked round Fleet Street, though not by me; and shortly after in London and in some provincial papers the same idea almost exactly was worked up by other people.

Can you sell such a series to the *Star* or one of your papers? Try it Primmy. Use your wits about how to present the proposal. Do anything you like with my material. I got the editor first and he arranged for the visits. It was great fun. I was almost fêted: civic cars, and launches for the harbour thing. . . . Get the *data*, even if you can't use it before you leave Toronto—the local names and statistics which would enable us to change the stuff into Toronto, if you are here before you do your write-up. But do it there if you've time—and the dollars are yours, please. . . .

Hope you're well darling. So glad I'll be seeing you soon   —Love, John.

But that kind of journalism was not for her—partly, I suspected, because she knew that even if commissioned to undertake it she dared not risk the physical strain of all-night work such as it involved—but certainly because, as she told me in reply, there was no place for it in local newspapers or radio programs. As vehicles for writing of even that degree of seriousness she had dismissed them in derisive contempt.

When, at the close of that letter of January third, I had said, "So glad I'll be seeing you soon," I was doubtfully keeping up a pretended confidence that I might indeed be doing so. But the doubt and the pretence evaporated when, toward the end of January, I had a wholly unexpected legacy from an elderly lady who had aspired to write and to whom I had given for a time professional help. It was not a large legacy, but large enough to work as if by magic an instant transformation in outlook for me. It could pay for an Atlantic crossing, bringing Babs to me; or, if illness or other circumstances prevented that, taking me to her in Canada. I knew that her book-reviewing and her exhausting pre-Christmas job of selling books had been undertaken to provide money enough to pay her way back to me without having to depend for it on her family. Knowing that dependence on her family irked her more and more I wrote inviting her to make use of my windfall legacy, offering to send the whole amount of it to be added to whatever she had earned. She was touched and grateful; but, with ominous significance I felt, she did not hurry to book a passage on an early sailing. On the contrary she clearly intended to postpone still further her return to me, to stay in Toronto and press on with writing her book of hospital reminiscences, the real, rooted writing of which I knew her to be capable and which I had once urged her to do.

50 Forest Hill Road
Toronto
Monday, 24 February, 1936.

John, my darling:

Do you know, at lunch today Bep [her well-to-do stepmother] talked of selling some stock to have some money to buy a new car—pay for some trips—send Babs to England if she wants to go. I was touched by that. In a burst of gratitude I nearly—but not quite, you notice—made her a present of my plans. I nearly said to her, "I'll go, and I may never come back. But if I come back, unattached, I'll come back very soon, and after that the British Isles are washed out for me for evermore. And *anyway* I'll never live here again [Forest Hill Road]. . . . I am slogging grimly on at the stuff for my book. I've sixteen pages of typewritten notes now—memories called up by lecture notes, ward notes, patients' names, treatments, etc. Mountains of it. The Junk Shop is full of such mountains. I have managed to lash myself down to a desk for a few laborious hours at least. When you're in a black, destructive, what-the-hell mood, look at the devastating, laboured rubbish you write! I'm in no spirit to preserve a *line*! I'd make a bonfire of most of my life cheerfully.

Darling—this letter-writing business—you have revolted against it all the way along haven't you? Bite on it a little longer, only a little longer. . . . So long, darling   —Babs.

A few days later she wrote suggesting that the "little longer" might be only a few weeks longer, to first or second April. It is a letter so evocative of the mood, place, time—the *feel*, of all that turbulent, crucial passage in our lives that I quote from it at some length, and—that its references may be understood—I turn back to quote, also at some length, from my letter to her of 19 and 20 February, to which hers is in reply. First my letter:

68 Campbell Park Avenue
Belfast
Wednesday, 19/2/36, 10.45 PM

I'm getting deeper and deeper sunk and stuck in this wretched Belfast rut, darling. This forenoon I heard an interesting-looking roundsman hollering out his wares, "Coal Bricks!" as he passed my window. I hailed him. Brought him in. Took down his "story." Made a script of it. Went down to BBC. Showed it. Sold it, for broadcast on Saturday evening—one of those programs, the only one, that is kept open till almost the day of transmission. I spent Monday evening in the fearfully dingy and overcrowded kitchen of a slum quarter—hearing a "band"—some young men pathetically trying to do something with themselves by playing a weird combination of mouth-organs, fiddles, guitars, etc. It is part of the work of getting "characters" for low-life, dead-end programs. I like those fellows—though I know them too well to sentimentalize or idealize them. I get on well with them, too. Which I count to my credit.

I was after an idea I had of putting a whole back street—actually as it is, not acted from a studio by actors—on the air. I got hold of a real rascal of a fellow from a likely back street, got him into a pub, bought him some drinks, and soon had him telling me who lived in that street and what they do. An interesting gang. Gipsies camp there on a To Let plot. There's a band. A lot of characters of the very sort I was after. When I got him out of the pub with a plan to meet me later and take me into the den of not-such-dreadfully-black iniquity, I went back to the pub telephone, rang up the BBC's Variety Producer, told him enough to make him say he'd wait for me—and round I went slightly intoxicated by my idea as well as the idea-working alcohol. The V.P., whom I then met for the first time, fairly brightened up at what I told him of my plan. I asked for a battery of microphones to plant in that street one evening, and for his approval of my going right ahead with making an "actuality" show of it. Half an hour later I walked out with the desired "Go right ahead." And I think that V.P. is going to be a friend. I got on with him, too!

Boasting? Well, darling, if I can't boast a bit to you—who the divil else am I to boast to? Damn it I don't want to boast to anyone else. But on reflection—the curse on this "reflecting!"—I know how little it means in money and how much in time and work. Only I felt glad to have pulled it off.

And *that's* what I mean by getting stuck here. I can't start a thing like that and then run off to London and leave it. And I hate being here—though the weather is like spring, and the country around is lovely.

I'll start no more hares in this field, I think. If I do I'll be here till summer. Better if I could do the same kind of stunt in London. Better pay. Better everything. But there's peace here. I'm loath to join battle in the "jungle" till the last possible moment. But I think I really must get over soon. I'll let you know.

And darling I haven't touched F. P. (a planned relocating of my play *Family Portrait*) for Flora Robson. Tyrone Guthrie is in New York. He comes back at the end of March. He is in the same theatrical set as Flora Robson, and he also is interested in F. P. I was told—by Bertie Scott, voice-production wonderman to Flora Robson and for Guthrie at the Old Vic—that I would be a fool not to strain every brain-cell to get the script ready for those two by the end of March. I think I am nearly ready to tackle it. One morning I'll fling everthing else on the floor and barge right through with it. You'll know I'm at it when the postman brings you nothing but "lines"—all hisses and scratches. You'll think, "Is this his idea of getting himself into 'fine, gay, fighting trim' for me!" And you'll want to keep out of my way.... Maybe you'd be wise!

Am I at it already, do you think? Arrogant. Aggressive. That's how I am this minute. It's absurd. Or—is it alcohol? Primmy, goodnight to you. I'm for bed.

Friday, 21/2/36. 2 PM

I have just reluctantly complied with your "please John, burn this," and put the first of the two "Bremen" letters on the fire. A pity, in one way, for it was an important letter. [It contained a bitter outburst against what she felt as intolerable constraints of continued life at home.] These are good letters in themselves, and they record a bit of your life and mine which is vital to us both. But I see your point. I, who have never hoarded anything, am incapable, just yet, of reacting in my otherwise normal way and scrapping anything that comes from you the moment it has done its work of carrying me your message. It is one of love's lunacies that even the string you've tied round a parcel seems precious and not to be thrown away—but I've had at least sufficient sense of humour not to act the loon to *that* extent. I could carry all my belongings in a couple of suitcases. So it has always been with me. So it will remain. But your letters I will keep for the present anyway—unless you say "please John, burn them." Reasonable beings? Bah! We don't reason. We merely react, and then dig out reasons to justify our reactions.

I found that letter lifting me right into Toronto and into Forest Hill Road. I've been there, now. I like your father, if you won't think it impertinent of me to say so. . . . I am afraid, though, that my whole background and values—on the social and political and other not-personal levels—are too different from his own. All the same I hope he will see me at Forest Hill, one day, for I would love to spend awhile looking at you in your own environment, as you say. And I mean to drift around Dahwamah with you, lying back in the Olivia [her canoe] and watching you paddle up into the gleam of moon or sun. Oh darling, if that should be possible, before too late for vivid response to such loveliness, possible in peace and acceptance and easy freedom, I should put the scales down with a thump on the credit side and know that life for me had weighed down at last with excess of good.

Ah, I know you. I know you to the deep core of your being because in those deepest things I was not mistaken. We count good and ill by the same tokens. On superficial things—all the every day *liaison* parts—we will certainly be liable to blazing disagreements. You have a basketful of crotchets to my pennyworth; you bother disliking disagreeable things and people more than I do; you feel deeper attachments and deeper repugnances, and you are consequently jealous and even, I think, a troublesome bit possessive in your affection compared with me. This, on the personal level. On the intellectual level—or rather where ideas are in question—you are fairly tolerant, I think, as compared with me. I feel ready to burn a fellow at the stake for something he says or thinks—you would loathe him for what you feel him to be. So I would enjoy the visit to your environment for it would not be necessary to mention what I thought or to ask what anyone else thought.

The round of your circle there—you ask, "Would you hate it . . . or be, temporarily, too grateful that we were together to care a damn?" "Temporarily"—well thought of darling. I would be grateful beyond anything anyone could say or do or be to make me otherwise. Don't you know I'd go round with you, and be opposite you at those "exquisite dinners," under one roof with you, secretly chortling. I'd be so careful of what could be seen—by anyone else but you—when our eyes met! The chortling would of course be for nothing but the joy of being with you.

So I will come. That is, I will come soon or later if fortune isn't bleakly against us. When, is a different question.

You say your father and your sister Jimmy feel distracedly that they will never see me if I don't come now. It is quite possible. For, later, they may not want to see me; though that would be because I had been traduced. (By some echoes from the London "jungle.")

Look now, Primmy; I agree with you, for the moment, that you had better come over here, first. You and I must take responsibility for our decision. And I agree—over here, with only the Jimmy Sleator "jungle" to consider— it will be straightforwarder. I am not at all sure that you yourself really want to go through and marry. We can decide that here. If yes—we can do it in our own way. Neither of us wants any of the orange-blossom, bridal-veil-

and-Wedding-March damn foolery. If no—then we can at least be near each other when we've a mind to. If we decided "yes" and it became clear that the "jungle" was bent on frustrating us—then it would have to be in Belfast, and quick and quiet. Then let adjustments work themselves out around the *fait accompli*. The whole immediate point is, while I am still in Belfast and you in Toronto I don't think the "jungle" war will show itself. Therefore for this letter, and for the next two or three letters, probably, I can say nothing more than has been said. You and I are not family-circle "marrieds" or ever likely to be: the marrieds-visiting-other-marrieds which you say you dread. I should loathe it and to hell with it just as quickly as you. We are and will always be what we were when we met; and if we marry or don't marry or no matter what, we'll not submit to any kind of life or any sort of friends but such as we already know to be *ours*. So you'll be all right.

I could live happily with you in Toronto. We could make our own life and live it by our own rules. But if I go out there I had better go out as your husband. Then there could be no discussion and everyone would at heart be relieved of the duty and responsibility of deciding. I'd probably make the grade with your people and they'd be glad to have you near them. But for me to go out to see you and them, and be seen by them like a highly respectable citizen paying suit for a wife—why, that's absurd in our circumtsances. And it simply wouldn't come off. I mean, *that* way, we just wouldn't get leave to marry, or anything else. So you see, capitalizing on our marriage—new clothes for you, fun for the Joy children, all the whoopee and whillabaloo—it really is not a possibility. So, say goodbye to that, and come on.

You were pretty funny about Mrs. Mair, all right! (A Belfast friend, whose insistent eagerness that I should, with her help, find and furnish a room and marry Babs, Babs resented.) But those things straighten out for anyone with sense. Don't think I'm likely to go furnishing a room under Mrs. Mair's direction. I'm as chary of being managed as you are—unless when I want to be managed. See?

I'm feeling like fighting now, as you may perceive.

Let's blather no more for now. Blather no more about love. Let's meet. Then it will be all right. If it ain't—it will be because we don't want it to be. So what's the use of going "white in the head?" I'd answer, "Well, dye it then." If I bother much more with this idiot problem I shall presently be at least well-thinned.

Primmy, for sheer devilment I told the Bangor Drama Club (whom I had addressed on "After Dinner Theatre") —half of whom were parents or morons, half young and amusing—"Let's eat, drink and commit adultery, for tomorrow we dye our hair." The old birds gaped, and the young ones laughed; and I remarked that evidently it was as true now as when Oscar Wilde first said it, that "the younger generation has absolutely no respect for dyed hair."

Yours splenetically   —John.

PS, in post office. But darling I'm not really feeling so savage as this may suggest. Did you think I was?

That continuing vacillation about the if and the when of our reunion—a worrying will-o'-the-wisp glimmering between the lines of all her letters—was evident again in her reply; or I seemed to detect it there despite the definite date given at the end.

50 Forest Hill Road
Toronto
Monday, 2 March, 6.10 PM

John my darling I am *miserable*, thank you. I *feel* like laying my head on your shoulder and I am going, as you see, to do so. No consideration for *you*, 3000 miles away and quite helpless to do anything about it, is going to stop me. I feel it would relieve my feelings to lie face down and *bellow*. What is it all about? I don't know. It is an accumulation of misery. It is partly, I think, that I hate myself. I think—in film jargon—that I could put on a top hat and walk under a snake. I have been working up to this pitch-black mood for weeks, and now here it is. . . . Here is where you should be. Ah, darling, what would I *give* to have this particular evening unbroken with you! *Now*. For at this moment I would talk. I would spill the whole bag of tricks at your feet, and say *look*! The result might be disastrous, but of course I am lulled to an easy confidence that you would whitewash it *somehow*, magician fashion, and pick me up out of the ruins and comfort me.

Father and Elizabeth [Bep, her step-mother] are not going now [to Sea Island Beach, Georgia] till Saturday. My heart sank when it was put off. For I had been counting on this empty house to restore my sanity. I feel so—dead—so at odds with myself that I long to be alone. I miss Father badly when he goes, but I am no fit company for anyone.

Tuesday, 10.20 AM

What I think really started me off on this was your letter, Wednesday the nineteenth, 10.45 PM, and Friday the twenty-first, 2 PM. It was a little bit of a sock in the jaw wasn't it, darling? Here and there, anyway. *Quite* deserved, as I humbly and immediately admitted. I am lonely for you, and distracted and miserable and *bored*, so that the most lightly aimed sock in the jaw has a good chance of laying me out. Darling, we are both of us at the end of our endurance over this. For myself I don't think letters are going to solace me much longer. I need to *do* something about it. You must see what a state I'm in that the need of a decisive step appeals to me!

119

I liked your antics with the amateurs [Bangor Drama Club] though I felt sorry for them, wilting under it. Did you feel better after you had gone for them all? On Saturday afternoon—this has become an institution—I collected Chips [terrier dog] from Montclair, and then went on to Glencairn [the Joys' house] where I picked up Weekes [terrier dog] and Howard. It was a glorious day though the wind across the snow-bound fields was still very cold. The snow was lovely. Soft, untrampled, light as feathers, and dazzling white. For the first time the creeks were unfrozen, and you could see running water flowing darkly between the overhanging, crumbling banks of snow. Howard and I hung over the little bridges, fascinated, watching it move again. This is *our* first hope of spring. Roads are blotted out and bushes buried in snow, yet. By the time we reached the Market we were glad to get in and feel the Turkish-bath heat instead of the icy wind. It was crowded in there, and we had no intention of buying anything so we speedily tired of this entertainment. I thought what fun it would be if one *was* buying the week's supplies, because the things looked so deliciously fresh and promising.

Then we found the coffee stall and regaled ourselves on "red hots," doughnuts, coffee for me, lime rickey for him, and started home. Every week now the sunset is later, but I love watching it dye the snow.

The Joy family—to bed. I read the children a chapter of *Mary Poppins*. Then, alone downstairs, I smashed the lump of coal until I had a blazing fire. Then I pulled up the sofa, turned out the lights, and lay there, with a couple of very jealous dogs keeping watch on each other, half-asleep. The only thing that casts a shadow on this imitation of paradise, dreaming in the firelight after hours in sun and wind, is that it cannot go on forever.

I think your idea of "low-life" programs is grand. . . . I hope you have a knock-out success with it, for you *should*.

I don't wonder the Variety Producer brightened up. He might well. Oh, I wish I could hear it, though. I see that is going to keep you in Belfast; but you loathe the idea of wading into the London morass any sooner than you have to, don't you? You would gladly put it off for ever, wouldn't you? I don't blame you—and I am frightened of it *for* you —especially without me.

Darling *write* that play for Guthrie and Flora Robson. I see it going clean over the top. I see *us* sitting on top of the world because of it. . . . Oh, I should expire with pride. And I am too far away to be withered by your exasperation at these excursions into fancy! I shall continue the iniquitous practice of dreaming. . . . The postman may bring me nothing but "lines"—all—was it all kisses, hisses or misses? —and scratches. I do *hope* kisses! But the general tone of the letter is *not* promising!

Thank you, darling, for burning the one I told you to burn. I'm glad that you *don't* feel like feeding them to the blaze—"for the present anyway." I don't want to write to you another instant. I want to be *with you*. Funnily enough I feel as if we'd weathered the gale up *to* January, and since then had been going to bits. There was some point in saying —and clinging to—January.

I am not worried about you and my family liking each other. I know the answer—you would. . . . You'd want to be with them and they'd want you—both feelings having nothing to do with me. And we must contrive that Dahwamah business. Not "this year, next year, sometime . . ." but this year *or* next year.

As far as your analysis of *us*—I don't know. You may be right. I think I'd come to life again with you. It's not in my power to pay you a greater compliment. Egotistical. I know!

You are *sweet*, darling, the way you let me rage and fume and kick and bite and scratch—and continue as if there had been no fireworks! It makes me quite hopeful of our future

—if not for my ultimate soul! You are very soothing, did you know?

And I was touched by your saying you could be happy living in Toronto with me. Bless you, you know *nothing* about it. You just mean you'd be happy living with me, and I must confess I rather yearn for it. My imagination falters at giving them, and this (family and family circle) up *for life*.

"This idiot problem," you say. Is that what it is now? I took what comfort I could out of your "PS, in Post Office." I couldn't afford to be sunk by a broadside from you when I was already practically drowned in despair! "Let's blather no more about love," you say. Eh? All right, all right. I'll come over the first or second week in April, *if* it's possible. And as far as I can see, it will be. Where do I come to— London? And do we decide *stat* then, at once, what we'll be doing?

So long, then, my lunatic. Not a *word* of love. But you know I think it would be nice if you wrote me one of the best —immediately.

Are you still anxious to knock me down and walk on me? I felt you were. So I was glad of the PS.

Yours dejectedly   —Babs.

What covert purpose, what hopes or plans, simmering half-consciously in Babs' mind but—perhaps with careful deliberation kept from me—could be inferred from that "whole bag of tricks" which she would spill at my feet and say *look*! though "the results might be disastrous"? And inferred, too, from that "*if*" pinned to her promise, "I'll come over the first or second week in April—*if* it's possible." But we were entirely at one in feeling that letters were not going to solace us much longer; that we had been right in fixing January as the end of our separation, and that since January we had both "been going to bits." Yet now we were nearing

April, and still that tantalizing "*if*"!

Reflecting constantly on all this unsettled and worried me; yet I thought best to avoid as far as possible speculating on what I was not being told. I would press on as if I had no doubt at all that we were soon to be together again, married or not—or else, what to me loomed darkly as the death-in-life alternative, be lost, lost to each other—permanently.

> 68 Campbell Park Avenue
> Belfast
> 16/3/36

Thank you, my dear, for your letters which came this afternoon when I was in the act and parcel of throwing down my pencil after a slog which began at eight o'clock in the morning—slog at the play, the reconstruction of the original F. P. for Lennox Robinson and Guthrie—not the Mayfair version for Guthrie and Flora Robson. Scott came back from London yesterday morning—he returns again tomorrow—and he told me Flora had asked him where was that Irishman and his play? She said Guthrie would be back from New York in ten days—and if my play were forthcoming and anything like up to what she imagined it might be, she wanted it, to look at, at once. So I'm despatching F. P. number 1 (the revision of the original Ulster back-street version). I *must* get it out of my mind, off the stocks, first. I couldn't *do* the Mayfair one, at the moment anyway. Not if a keg of gold were waiting sure, on the moment of Finis. Something's blocking my mind from working in terms of Mayfair . . . and anyway if Guthrie and Flora Robson read the Ulster version and are impressed—that's something.

So much for me. Now, you. Two stories, "Fowls of the Air" [her to-order story about a woman air-pilot] and "Give me Henry" [another to-order, both for the Toronto *Star Weekly*], $50. Babs, you're doing it! I'll drown an extra sprig of shamrock for you tomorrow, St. Patrick's Day.

You ask if I meant *h*isses in what I said about my "lines all hisses and scratches." Hisses it was, not kisses. But darling if I had you near me now I'd kiss you till you swooned.

Must go to bed. Fare thee well, five hours back, 3000 miles away! Do you think we *may* meet, some day again? It seems incredible. But so did the crocuses and daffodils a month ago.

St. Patrick's Day

That was a silly bit of burbling to you last night. "Kiss you till you swooned!" Lord, the idiocy of writing it down! Doing it—ah, that's a different affair. But, never mind, darling—we might have spilled that sort of pitiful slop over a lot more of our letters. And now it's near an end. Why, a fortnight tomorrow—April! April Fool's Day! . . . Coming, Southampton? I'll be seeing you?

Get all the sun and all the tang and tan of the ocean, every day when you're coming over. Me—I'll be a worn and pallid relic—surviving—merely surviving. Where shall we go, when you come over? What shall we do? A week's tramping together, by ourselves. Go-as-you-please, through Sussex? Nothing planned. Just a few things with us—the rest dumped somewhere—anywhere—a railway cloakroom. Maybe we'll finish at my sister's new home in Seaford. But I think better fix no rigid plan. A week utterly free of everybody and everything, just wandering off and here and there, the two of us together. That's my only plan. The rest can wait and work itself out.

I have just turned down a contract to broadcast from here —Belfast—third week in April—tennis. It's no good evading this need to cut out hanging about here after odd bits and scraps. I'll see what can be forced out of London. You'll be safe for a month or two. So shall I. After that—who can tell? But we'll have had that month or two, at least. And you say you'd "come alive again" with me. Well, if Fate plays right for us, this spring is going to make the rest, before and after, worthwhile.

So, come to me brown as an Indian; come gaily, freely, serene and—and just as you were . . . to keep me still adoring you—your gentle mockery keeping me challenged and alert—your foolish faith in me making me wonder can there be something in it not so foolish after all. So, just *come*, my darling; for I *am* tired of having you and not having you. Having you 3000 miles away is worse than not having you at all. And if you go away from me again, then:

Closed the shutters
Barred the door
Since I shall not see your face
Nor be held in your embrace
Hear no chiding word nor word
Praising what I've done or said.

I shall say: Goodbye, my dear. I loved you. I've lost you. And now I doubt if there are any odd bits and scraps of myself lying around and worth picking up.

For it *has* been a shattering affair, don't you think?
—Love from John.

As April approached I cabled to Babs that by April first I should be in London and would meet her at Southampton. What boat? What sailing? But by April first I still had no word of boat or sailing. On March thirtieth, a letter written by her on March nineteenth brought but another cry of exasperation. "Are you cross, darling? God knows you aren't to be blamed—by me—if you have arrived at the boot-throwing stage. I passed it some time ago. A fatal calm has settled down on me instead . . . I am as blank of helpful statements as a soothsayer, and *their* ignorance of my future is as dark as mine." A letter written four days later but which reached me only on April sixth, contained the first hint that our April Fool's Day reunion might not, after all, take place.

50 Forest Hill Road
24 March, 1936

I wonder what we'd have been like if we'd been together this last awful drag-end of the winter. Like the Kilkenny cats? Do you think we're in this furious mood because we've tired ourselves beyond endurance over this? My old diaries are nothing but crêpe, gloom, tears, end-of-life. It's over though, isn't it? I am still fearful. I've never yet said definitely it is over. Neither you nor I, however we may bluff, see far beyond the exact moment. . . .

When you come here you'll see what I mean when I say that you don't put an ocean between you and what you've left behind—you exchange one life for another. . . . The end of this purgatory? . . . I have never really, believingly, pictured the end of this—our meeting somewhere. More readily I picture impossibilities, like your opening the door there and just walking in, smiling as if you'd slain a dragon or so, and—here you were!

In about two days time Father and Elizabeth will be home again. Sunday, April fifth is Father's birthday. "I may be gone before you come back," I said to him, to see what would happen. "You mustn't go before my birthday," said Father. Well, then they'll say, "Spend Easter Sunday [April twelfth] here—it is either that or spending it on the ocean." Not that it matters a continental *where* it's spent of course.

Everyone circles warily round what happens after I go. What I do, I mean. Father and I avoid the sad details. . . .

So long then, darling. The end of this purgatory? Yes, it will be soon. And then? Never mind the answer — Babs.

But was there another more serious reason for Dr. Primrose's fatherly wish that on his birthday Babs should not be on the ocean? The answer came in the form of a wild cry of despair which, though written on April ninth, reached me in London after that day on which I had hoped to be on the dock at Southampton, waving welcome as the liner with Babs aboard slowly moved in.

50 Forest Hill Road
Toronto
Thursday, 9 April

Oh John, I am simply beside myself! How *could* this happen? How did I let such a disaster creep up on me? Why didn't I swallow buckets of some quack medicine that would have choked off the cough? Why didn't I do a bolt while they were gone? In the name of sanity what have I been thinking of?

And this letter will take so long getting to you. And you will, within a few hours, have that *loathsome* cable—and like me you will be dazed by the catastrophe. I can't talk sense. I can do nothing but wring my hands and cry about it. It just can't have happened. I just have dreamed this last business.

Well, it *has* happened.

Here are the facts—the full account to supplement that beastly cable. I saw Dr. Parfitt [the TB specialist] yesterday. I've been coughing for six weeks, but it didn't sound like anything but a throat cough. He announces today from a mess of X-rays, blood tests, stethoscopes and what not, that I have an active lesion in my right lung; that it's sloughing away and must be stopped. I said instantly that it was all very unfortunate, but I had to get back to England, lung or no lung.

Madness. Suicide. Permanent injury. Crocked for life—
and so on. Father looking worried to death.

Finally, unconvinced and champing with rage, I agree to
let Parfitt do a pneumothorax—let air into lung cavity—
collapse bad lung—gives it a rest and stops it disintegrating.
This, he says, if all goes well, may let me travel in four
weeks' time. To this I cling like a drowning rabbit. *In four
weeks' time.* I have tried hard to be philosophical: to say,
"Oh well you weren't going till after Easter—this is *only*
putting it off two weeks. But it's hard. John, my darling,
promise me we'll be together *soon. Swear* it instantly, or I
shall go right off the deep end. And when we are together
—listen darling—they can go and blow themselves up with
their old pneumos for all I care. Once I get out of this jam
I am never, never, *never* going to have anything to do with
the medical profession again. Oh God, how ungrateful! I
mean if they are really saving me from years of misery.

Well, I don't know what I am writing. I am distracted
with it all.

My poor John, to have this hurled at you. Oh how *cruel*
it is anyway! I have let you down badly about letters this
week—but I didn't care because I'd got my ticket for
the *Berengaria* and thought a little space with no letters
wouldn't worry you at all.

I have four letters from you—but I can't read any of
them without wanting to cry. They're *not* true anymore.
They don't know this horrible, last, diabolic, spoke in the
wheel. I am sitting in the Junk Shop nursing this last bomb-
shell, and I am all alone. Who could have *believed* anything so scurvy would happen to us? Hasn't enough risen
up and smote us? What *are* we asking for that the whole
army of fate should want to get us down?

Don't expect anything better of me tonight darling. Just
let me cry on your shoulder, and weep and rant and kick for

128

all I'm fit. Don't attempt to argue or philosophize. Tomorrow—tomorrow I may be coming to the surface again. I *loathe* this pneumo business. I wanted to come to you so fit, walking on air—even tanned if I could, and radiant.

Well, my dear darling John, here it all is. I can't make it any better, my darling. I would if I could. I *have*, I suppose, sprung a little leak in my lung, and I will *have* to do what they say. I feel wearily—oh God, let me get over in my month—let us be together in a month and I will overlook this last preposterous tax on our patience. Anyway darling, don't imagine I'm very ill, or any nonsense of that sort. When you *do* see me—when at last I slip out of these chains and trot down the gangplank into your widespread arms—you'll say: "You fraud and humbug! No-one ever looked so fit." And I will say, "In the name of sanity hang on to me—hang on to me *tight*, and stand for no nonsense."

So long darling. I am—as you will have grasped—*upset!* But never mind—we'll get there *yet* —Babs.

For this black news I had been prepared by that "*loathsome* cable." Though sent by Babs on April eighth it had not reached me until April tenth. This was Good Friday. I was staying at Seaford with my sister and her husband, Annie and Jack Carson. It had told me:

DARLING HAVE SPRUNG A LEAK IN ONE
OF MY LUNGS REMAINING HERE FOR
TREATMENT FOR FOUR WEEKS WILL
THEN COME OVER TO YOU SICK WITH
DISAPPOINTMENT AT DELAY BLESSINGS
ALLOAH BABS

And I had at once cabled sympathy and encouragement. But because of all that I had known of this illness, particularly of Middleton Murry's anguished experience of it with

Katherine Mansfield and Violet, I took several days to steady myself, facing all it involved as I walked on the Downs, discussing it with Annie and Jack, setting my course.

The Weald. Grove Road
Seaford. Sussex
14/4/36

Well, darling, so here I am, starting the letter-writing all over again, when I thought I'd be walking with you over the Downs. But this isn't a complaint. I know that the doubt and difficulty of this jam have knocked you out in the cruel way your cable said. I do blame myself. I ought to have had gumption and self-control enough to prevent the jam happening. Still, it has happened, and now all I want is that you should have peace and be able to get well quickly.

I hope you have written telling me truly and fully how you are—and that you will keep on doing that. I am in doubt, and the doubt is hard to bear. I naturally imagine you have been trying to let me down lightly, though I warned and begged you—last "whirlpool" time—not to conceal anything of that kind from me. Don't do it, Babs. Do let me be certain I know just how you are and what is happening. I am not too silly or too soft to be told. I want you to trust me fully. I have reserves of stoic fortitude on which you can count to see me through any stress like this.

On Thursday I came here. Cold, wintry Easter. There were thick banks of primroses on the railway cuttings, coming down. I thought I'd be putting a bunch into your hands, one of these days. And now . . . ! Never mind. Have faith and courage to be yourself and accept what comes with the gay spirit that's you and that I love. Emotional disturbance and perplexity get you down. But there is nothing worth the kind of state into which fear of this situation and its possible consequences has swung you. What the deuce are you destroying yourself for? I ask you to try to take the whole thing coolly for it is certain everything can and will sail into serenity and sanity if only you are willing to trust yourself completely to whatever may be coming. Let it come. Let it simply come, Babs. Don't be anxious, or in a hurry, or trying to force the gates.

This sounds hysterical, I suppose. It is what I have found it necessary to say to myself. . . . I will do anything to make you happy when you are with me again. When that will be, I don't know. But don't be afraid. You are going to be all right. . . . And whatever comes or goes—whatever you do or don't do—I think you the same adorable Babs

—Love from—John.

She had that cable of sympathy and encouragement with her when writing from the Medical Arts Surgery. "Here," she said, "they plunge various needles into me, and pump air into my lung." I imagined it to be a fearful and a recurring ordeal. But she said she bore it because she had been persuaded that "in three weeks and four days" she'd "be shot of it all and sailing from New York." She promised, "I'll cable you, telling you my boat." Then, in her letter of the next day, in what she described as "a whirlpool of ecstasy," she wrote, "Listen, my darling John. Listen— listen at last to something worth hearing! Are you ready? My white-haired tyrant, the vainest man that ever put blueing in his hair-wash, has just said that I can make reservations on the *Berengaria* sailing from New York on May eighth." She would at last soon be on her way. But on the following day she had fears. She wrote, "He raises various horrific bogeys to frighten me. If I should elect to have pleurisy—a common thought with pneumos, apparently— I couldn't go. But I'm clinging to their rules—rest, quiet— for grim death. I scarcely breathe lest the train to New York on the night of the seventh May. . . . But we won't think of it." As the end of April drew nearer she reported: "I can detect in the air a strong current of opposition to my going in two weeks. Father has been diplomatically begging me to consider staying another two weeks longer so as to have those two weeks for going about after these four in bed. Poor Father! He said 'I am thinking of John, too. After all —to risk your whole future health!' So, as to getting aboard the *Berengaria* on the eighth, I am menaced by two cross-currents: this pleurisy business ... and Father's vote, strong and steady for two weeks longer. That's why I didn't cable you my sailing, darling. I want nothing to go wrong after that cable goes."

It was gradually becoming clear to me that, at whatever cost to my work and my prospects of work I must act on the conviction that the emotional stress of all the uncertainties and postponements was the cause—or at least the precondition—of this deadly renewed onset of TB. To allay it I must be prepared to drop everything I was doing and go out to be with Babs in Canada, for as long as I dared on my perilously limited means. I sent her a cable telling her so, and wrote, saying so more fully.

Raglan Hotel
Up. Bedford Pl.
London, WC
24/4/36
... Tomorrow morning I'll probably know whether to send any more letters or not. But if you are held up ... if you are too unwell to risk coming to me I'll come over to you. I am sure you are right—that nothing will be so sure to gather you back to security and peace and your own darling gay self as US—our being together again. So, come what may, go what may, we'll contrive it. I put that now as the greatest need: for you an urgent and perhaps decisive need: for me something I want and need more than any other thing in life—and I will act accordingly ... I simply

132

had to go down to Piccadilly to send you that—perhaps rather indiscreet—cable. But the thought of you risking any particle of your strength so as not to disappoint me—I simply could not bear it. A little more and I should have been on the *Berengaria* myself, or on some less luxurious boat. Yet Parfitt and your father and sister and the others are right, must know the risk. They would think my cable an impertinence, perhaps. You won't. To them I would apologize. You will understand. You will not be flurried by it, I hope.

You once asked, "What do you suppose means peace and safety and victory for me?" I know, I know; and it will not be denied you if anything in my power can avail for us. . . . I count all else of no moment whatever. So long then, my dear   —John.

PS. Today a series of scripts for feature programs about the Home Counties was practically commissioned from me. I could *write* them anywhere. Must at once do prodigious research at the British Museum.

If the scripts mentioned in that PS as "practically commissioned" should in fact be commissioned, I saw the fees—when added to the small legacy I had received—as providing the means to go to Canada. Much turned on that. (Yet failing it I should have gone anyway—even if having to borrow to do so.) The thought behind my remarks, that I could write the scripts anywhere, and that I must at once do prodigious research for them, was that, the research being done, I could do the writing in Canada if the BBC would agree.

I did long to see Babs walk down the gangplank but not, as her father had cautioned, at risk of her whole future health. A wife in seriously and permanently impaired health would render life for both of us an unending and

133

finally unendurable desperation. So I was anxiously aware
that in the next few weeks much of what must shape my life
for years to come would be fashioned. Babs' letters were to
tell me of this, bulletin by bulletin.

9 Montclair Avenue
Toronto
Tuesday, 29 April. 7.07 PM

Darling your blessed cable arrived today. This morning
I was oversleeping deliberately—in a bad temper—in an as-
there-isn't-anything-to-wake-up-for-why-wake-up? frame
of mind. But there was your cable to wake up for had I only
known it! I'm sorry you've been worrying, darling. I suppose you couldn't very well help it. But I have *truthfully*
told you all I know, and I should think the very fact that I
am still coming would reassure you. . . . But this last super-
imposed and extra nightmare has undermined my calm
badly.

Long before you get this you will have had from the
cable its news. They don't want me to sail on the eighth,
though I am *quite all right*—and under much pressure I
have agreed to give it up till the next sailing of the *Berengaria*, which is on the twenty-eighth. Parfitt says the X-ray
shows some "adhesions," and he would like more time in
order to fill me up with more air. Oh, something like
that . . . I love you for saying you'd come—but I think not.
Not if I can manage it without any *risk*. . . . If I can't, I'll
cable. . . . Thank you for your letters—like your cable, I
bound up my shattered lung with them.

I am still in bed. I read mystery stories and do a prodigious amount of sleeping. I wake up in a dear little room
with sprigged wallpaper. I eat breakfast, semi-somnolent
and with unbrushed hair, and when I feel equal to it I make
up the old face . . . and go into the enormous bedroom-and-
sunroom. I lie on the chesterfield almost in the arms of the

134

apple tree which grows outside in the garden—a lazy, profitless life with all the hours there are to pine in. Write to me . . . help me *bear* this last exasperation. The twenty-eighth! Oh, when you get this—*not* so long!   —Babs.

But to me the prospect of yet another month of waiting *was* long. I saw the weeks until May twenty-eighth as interminably, unbearably long; and perhaps because unbearable it was beginning to generate in me a defensive feeling of unreality. I was unwillingly aware of a lurking skepticism however firmly I might say to myself and write to Babs that certainly this time she came to me or I should be on my way to her. As April turned into May I had from her a reassuring cable that she was "practically recovered."

Raglan Hotel
London, WC1
1/5/36

Well, my darling Babs—"Practically recovered" your cable said. I should like a cable every day. If I could afford it I'd prepay a daily one till you're quite well again. I have been slogging all day in the British Museum, on the material for the first of those—the Home Counties series. . . . I saw some verses an unknown poet of Rye wrote on a blank page in the town's archives, and in Henry VIII handwriting:

What greater gryffe may hope
Trew lovers to annoy
Than absente for to sepratte them
From their desired joye?

And thoughe the dystance of this place
Doe severe us in twayne,
Yet shall my harte they harte imbrace
Tyll we doe meete agayne.

Appropriate! —John.

50 Forest Hill Road
Toronto 5
Thursday, 7 May. About 6 PM
John my darling—my letters lately have been short, violent and incoherent. Very much *me*! Nor will this be much better. I am writing on my knee in the garden. It is hot, incredibly hot. All I have on—almost all—is a skirt, and a sky-blue sleeveless shirt. But my hair clings damply to my neck, and I think longingly of lakes and streams and green shade. It is 88 degrees. Yes, I thought you'd be surprised! Took for granted it was just the petulance of the convalescent? Well, it is not. Everyone is wilting. And I—am worshipping the warm breeze and sun-drenched air.

Well darling, although I have sat up to write to you I don't feel any great fluency coming on. My letters to you are over. They were only a bridge ever. Now they are nothing. I am engaged *altogether* in *coming*. Yesterday I came back—from Montclair—to Forest Hill, where Bep, characteristically, had roses in profusion, and rare foods and drinks, and a beach umbrella, and a chaise longue, imported to say Welcome. I am feasting my eyes on the garden, drinking in its greenness and the pale new leaves that feather the trees. Bep's stone fountain spangles the air, and a collection of birds come and bathe. And it is *warm*. A pleasant spot, Toronto, from now till November. I am *surrounded* with every comfort—every pleasing device. Alas, that it has always palled. This time it will have no chance....
I thought this morning—I wonder how long before John and I are pacing it out together, and I am showing him every single landmark. How long do *you* say? Perhaps I am only coming over to bring you home! So long my dearest lunatic. Aloha! —Babs.

That phrase, "only coming to bring you home," affected me, as when through a break in clouds one suddenly sees blue sky. Was that, perhaps, the ultimate aim, the bright hope, hidden but constant beyond all the obscure, drifting uncertainties? So that even if she managed to be aboard the *Berengaria* on May twenty-eighth it would not be to remain with me in London. I sent a note to her, saying, "I've made a sudden decision to cut away back to Belfast, not to return to London until the week beginning May twenty-sixth when I go down to Southampton to meet you." But I knew I was going home to do what should be needed if Babs should, after all, be disappointed in her hope that, "Perhaps 28 May will do me the honour of coming at my earnest request." I was going home to prepare for—and to tell my mother and sister about—a possible, and possibly prolonged, sojourn in Canada.

I cabled Babs that I was now in Belfast. She cabled back that she was getting well and would be on the *Berengaria*. Yet I went busily on every day, every evening, and far into the night seeking out and copiously noting new material about interesting characters of the back streets for the feature programs, *Ulster Echoes*, for BBC, and *Down Our Street* for "Belfast Evening Telegraph." My object was to provide myself with the makings of these features so that, if it chanced that I must indeed set out for Canada, I could write the scripts while there or on the way. It was a prophetic provision. Presently another cable from Babs brought the cry which resolved at last the question that for twelve months had distracted and tormented us—the if and when and where of our being together again. An agonizing consultation about her condition had led the TB specialists and her father to decide that, after all, she dare not without grave risk travel on May twenty-eighth, nor indeed, perhaps, for a lengthy time thereafter. Babs could not but submit. I cabled at once that I was coming. Then, thinking best to avoid aggravating tension by treating this decisive news and her acceptance of it as calmly as though it had been foreseen and expected, I wrote to her.

68 Campbell Park Avenue
Belfast
26/5/36

... What gorgeous weather it is here! All the flowers and flowering shrubs and trees are flinging themselves open-armed at the warm—the hot—sun. ... Your cable: in a way I was not surprised, darling. When you had told me in an earlier letter how you were sitting in your Forest Hill garden, in a skirt and sky-blue jumper and not much else— good of you to help me *see* you by those particulars—thinking of "streams and lakes and greenshade"—I thought—it isn't London, this summer! Dahwamah?

But I knew how cruel that final interview with the doctors must have been. I saw you, as your cable said, a "very wild Indian," and if I could then and there have transported myself over 3000 miles to you I'd have been walking in to hold you and comfort you. I am planning to sail as soon as ever I can disentangle myself from the programs and schemes for programs which I was carefully trying to get going for your coming—to pay the rent! Now it's Reverse! I feel like a sweating engineer down in the engine-room of a liner, who's been trying to force pace on her to get somewhere in unheard-of time—and suddenly he's all out, trying to halt, turn round, get back.

Don't take this as a grouse or reproof. It isn't. I really felt a sudden uprush of relief when I had cabled "Coming." I had feared, deeply, the effect on you of the voyage and the subsequent tensions of London. I was glad it was possible for you to stay awhile *and* to get to you. In a fortnight's time I'll be on my way. I don't care what, after that. But to think I'll be *with* you—with *you*! You showing me, as you

138

said, "every single landmark!"

I'm in a hurry to get back to London and get the minimum of preparation and adjustment made for the journey. I'm elated—in spite of the folly and danger, and all the rest of the important considerations that don't matter. We'll have that "bit" at last, eh? I can hardly bear the thought of it. It's too good, too good to be possible after all that has happened. Yet—it's ours—almost—already. Love to you, darling   —John.

Two days later she cabled again, and again I wrote:

68 Campbell Park Avenue
Belfast
29 May, 1936.

This morning your cable came, saying you feel happy now—now that it's settled—you staying—my coming. Happy. Well, that's what I wanted to hear. . . . It is worth anything, anything to hear of you swinging round to the light. *Be* happy, in your mind. Be well, Babs. . . . Probably I'll go over on the *Empress of Britain,* June sixth. But you'll have heard by the time you get this.

The BBC write today to say they like the Sussex program (my trial script for the Home Counties series). But they ask me to come to see them in Portland Place as soon as I get back to town. I will go over, try to fix up about as much work as I can, try to get the bones of the needed research—depending for the rest on the Toronto library—then over to you. . . .

So long, darling. I've finished writing letters. Can you read this handwriting? It merely says, "It's over. I'm coming. I'm glad." Till then   —John.

Having finished my work in such a whirl of rushing about, seeing people and taking notes as masked the sadness of leave-taking, I bade my mother and sister and Belfast friends farewell—a brief farewell, as I believed, since I thought that my stay in Canada must be limited to not more than three months. It was Whit Monday, June first. Back in London, to my gratification I found that the people at Broadcasting House were so pleased with the "Sussex" script that they commissioned the full series. But they were astonished and incredulous when I said, "But on Saturday I'm going to Canada from Southampton on the *Empress of Britain*." They thought I was joking. But I had booked passage and had my ticket, and they must have seen that my mood was far from one of joking. They said I couldn't do it. I had just signed a contract. When I told them enough of the reason that compelled me to go they were sobered and concerned and sympathetic, and saw that even in breach of contract nothing would stop me. They had tea brought in. We talked. I explained that every waking moment I already was and had been busy on research for the series, and offered to write the rest of the scripts in Canada and have them back in Broadcasting House by mail in time for rehearsal and performance. It was, they said, taking an unheard-of risk, but in the circumstances they agreed—on condition that before I left the ship at Quebec I should put into the ship's mail-box the script of "Surrey" which was to follow "Sussex," and that I should mail the remainder of the series at intervals of three weeks.

My last few days in London I spent intensely swotting from opening time until closing time in the British Museum, and then snatching a bit in some pub on the way to Foyle's bookshop in Charing Cross Road. There I found and bought to take with me some of the books I should need but had not time to search through at the British Museum and which, for aught I knew, might not be available in Toronto. Hectic partings from friends. Hurried buying of a few new things needed to make myself presentable: boots, jacket, cap, slippers, brushes. Frenzied packing-up. Saturday morning, June sixth. Breakfast at nine o'clock. The taxi. The drive to Waterloo as on that Saturday morning of parting almost exactly twelve months before: Hyde Park, Constitution Hill, the Palace, Birdcage Walk—but I was diverted from sentiments associated with those places by thoughts of letters I must manage to write on the short channel crossing aboard ship—there were fourteen of them, as well as copy of a song and two pieces of promotional blurb for the Home Counties Series I had promised to send to MacLurg at the BBC—all so as to catch the last post on the Cherbourg side of the Atlantic.

On arriving back in London several days earlier I had sent to Babs the last of that long, long sequence of heart-searing, exasperatingly inadequate written efforts to keep in touch—oh irony, in *touch*! Appropriately it was on a letter-card.

Raglan Hotel
Up. Bedford Place
London WC1. Tuesday, 2 June, 1936.

Well darling, here *is* the last of them—the letter-cards and the letters. You'll get this, I suppose, about Wednesday or Thursday next, and we'll be meeting on the tomorrow or next day—eh? Oh my dear I'm dreading, a bit, the shock your family are in for—you see I'm none the better for what's been happening these twelve months. Ten years older, or thereabouts. What's going to happen? No, don't think about it—yet. I'm elated, and sobered, by turns, at the thought that so soon I'll see you. I'm tired, a wee bit, after crossing with no sleep. But—oh Primmy, Primmy! My dear!   —John.

On that Belfast-to-Liverpool crossing I had not slept because of having, instead, to write a piece—on ventriloquism

—for *Ulster Saturday Night*; and because in doing so my overwrought brain seemed at times an echoing vault full of mock voices, whispering, teasing, confusing. On the channel crossing from Southampton I did manage to get the fourteen letters and the song and the blurbs into the mail at Cherbourg. In consequence I saw nothing whatever of departure or landfall; and this was already the pattern my days were to assume during the entire ocean crossing. What Christopher Fry was later to describe as "the boring excess of the Atlantic" had no chance to bore me, for all I saw of it was the heave and fall of the rushing water outside the porthole of my cabin, and the illimitable wilderness of it, mountains and valleys of it, threatening to engulf us beyond the slowly ascending and descending rail when once or twice a day I went up for a brisk walk and breather around the decks.

The ship's purser on hearing I was under obligation to write a script for the BBC and post it before we docked at Quebec, gave me for my sole use a four-berth cabin with a table in it for writing and typing. At meal times I heard of passing ships, of flotillas of spouting whales, of icebergs, of the sighting of land; but I had not dared to leave my cabin to see them, and did not see the St. Lawrence when we entered the great river—though nobody else did either because of dense fog, slowing the ship and distracting me by constant blasts on the fog-horn as I strove to finish my script. As we were drawing alongside the dock at Quebec I finished it, thrust it into an envelope and staggered with it to the ship's mail-box just as it was about to close.

I have written elsewhere—in my memoirs—of my sensations on first stepping ashore in Canada and on making the journey by rail from Quebec to Montreal to Toronto. Over the telephone at Montreal I heard Babs' voice again, pitched low in nervous excitement, tense and tremulous with diffidence and joy. When, at Toronto Union Station, burdened with suitcase and typewriter, I wearily emerged from the subterranean corridors and reached the barrier, she was there, waiting with her father and David Milne, his man. I felt they were as nervous as I, though I could hardly control the shaking of my limbs. Babs, in an elegant French summer coat of pinkish hue with hat to match, looked frail but lovely. She was leaning dependently on her father's arm, and as we turned to walk up the slight incline to the level of the entrance hall and the street I heard him quietly say, "Slow, Babs, slow." He may have intended it for me to overhear. I knew what was implied.

During the weeks which followed I had reluctantly to give much of my time to reading for and writing the next script of my series, "Middlesex." This I did in the pleasant garden Babs had described, sitting by the little fountain and shaded by the huge bright-coloured beach umbrella from the sun that all day long, day after day, was scorching the grass to the colour of straw. When the heat and glare became oppressive I moved to Babs' den, the Junk Shop at the top of the house. For the rest, Babs—her father having gone to Vancouver and her step-mother considerately leaving us as much as might be to each other—eagerly took me to visit house after house of her family and friends, all of them so welcoming and warmly hospitable that to my surprise the round of introductions was agreeably without embarrassment, and I could not deny Babs' delighted insistence that I was being a success.

There were frequent consultations—a first crucial one between Dr. Primrose and me before he went off to Vancouver. Others then, between Bep and Babs and me, and every day between Babs and me. Babs surprised me a little by questioning whether, after all, we should go through with it and marry. If we did—where? Toronto? And when? At once, before the family left Toronto to spend the summer at Dahwamah? Or later, after their return in September? They were to leave at the end of the first week in July. This havering continued until the beginning of that week. Then I brought it to an abrupt end by declaring: "We get married, and get married by the end of this week or I must go back at once to London." As I hoped and intended, Babs was relieved. She agreed that we would marry—on condition that each of us undertake never to hold the other if either wished to be free. The notion that either of us should ever wish to be free seemed to me preposterous, ridiculous. I laughed at it. But Babs—because of some old, obscure reluctance that she still deeply felt—was serious about it. So, since by the end of the week we were to marry, there began several days of most intense preparations— wedding clothes to be made—though not those of the white-veiled bride—a trousseau to be acquired, catering to be arranged, invitations to be sent out; for Babs, rather to my surprise though not at all to my displeasure, longed for the degree of dressing-up and celebrating that made it fun to be married by the fountain, under the shade of the enormous ancient oak tree in that garden.

Now it was as if transforming magic had touched her, banishing the wilting droop, restoring hope and confidence and spirit. She was again the Babs of our first times together in Regent's Park and Dorset Square—alight, springy, rising on her toes and laughing as she walked. I saw this, and wondered and rejoiced, regarding it as convincing evidence that the divided mind was whole again, free at last of the dreaded renunciation of family and friends and of Dah-wamah, free of the threatened ordeal of unknown conflicts and miseries in London.

Earlier in those weeks there had been other consultations, of a less exhilarating kind. The gravest of these took place in the Medical Arts Building, between me and the TB specialist Dr. Parfitt. This grim, white-headed ogre—as from his manner I then mistakenly regarded him—gravely told

144

me that for two years Babs could not safely travel, the pneumo-thorax injections of air into the collapsed lung must continue at brief intervals without risk of interruption, and if we should marry there must be no question of starting a child for at least three years after the TB had been stopped, which, encouragingly, he had no doubt at all that eventually it would be. He also admonished me that she must be kept in comfortable circumstances, and spared all avoidable anxieties and tensions. As he talked at me I watched his eyes and mouth and gestures, and felt he was rather enjoying it, the stern headmaster with the cane not quite concealed behind his back. But I suppressed as best I could the resentment and irritation which I felt.

July fourth—America's Independence Day, was to be known to Babs and me henceforth as Loss of Independence Day. We married, in the presence of the few friends who had not gone to their lake islands, and a few relatives who had purposely delayed going. It was high summer in the garden. Babs was delighted to have her two erstwhile "children"—her nieces Nancy and Sue Joy as bridesmaid and flower girl—and delighted that I had as best man her nephew Alex Joy.

For wedding-trip we were given as a present from Bep a week-long tour in a chauffeur-driven limousine—a circuit of that part of southern Ontario where various relatives of Babs lived, relatives to whom I was to be introduced and on whom we called. By Kingston, Montreal, Ottawa, Peterborough we came at last on Sunday morning the twelfth of July, with the Orange drums greeting us as we passed through every little township, to Dahwamah, the island that for Babs had been and was to remain for life " a place called Paradise."

Of our married life thereafter I have written in my memoirs, *In My Day*. I shall say, here, only that the cliché phrase "They lived happily ever after" was to prove for us, despite a full share of anxious struggle and illnesses and grief, simply and literally true. I cannot conceive how any two human beings could find in each other more profound, enduring, self-fulfilment and peace.

ENVOY

In 1941 Babs, writing retrospectively in her journal about "our bit"—that Elysian interval we had promised ourselves —said:

> No living soul has been so happy, so rooted and grounded in happiness as I have been these five blessed years.

It was a blessedness that was to endure through all the years that followed until 1971, when she died.